# Writing: Steps to Success
## Level 4 to 5 +

Kevin Eames  Karyn Taylor  David Trelawny-Ross
Consultant: Debra Myhill

Hodder & Stoughton

A MEMBER OF THE HODDER HEADLINE GROUP

Acknowledgements:
The authors and publishers would like to thank the following for their kind permission to reproduce copyright material:

Copyright Text:
ppix–x two extracts from English Text Mark Scheme © Qualifications and Curriculum Authority; pp7, 10–11,15–16, 18–19 all extracts from *Daz 4 Zoe* by Robert Swindells (Puffin, 1990) © Robert Swindells, 1990, reproduced by permission of The Penguin Group (UK); pp29–30 a newspaper article entitled *The riddle of the Hood* by Simon Crerar © Simon Crerar/Times Newspapers Limited, December 2001; p31 graphics © Times Newspapers Limited, December 2001; pp48, 50 a newspaper article entitled *Bad driving is the real killer* by Quentin Willson, which appeared in *The Mirror*, August 14, 2001 © Mirror Syndication International, August 2001; pp55, 58 a newspaper article entitled *Helpline needs doctoring*, which appeared in the *Daily Express*, August 6, 2001 © Express Newspapers, August 2001; p69 an online review of *The Fast and the Furious* by Adam Smith © Adam Smith/Empire Magazine/Planet Syndication; p71–72 the poem *A Case of Murder* by Vernon Scannell, reproduced with kind permission of the author.

Copyright Photographs/Graphics:
px Shell Island harbour © Dave Newbould; px Cave, with stalactites and stalagmites, Ogof Ffynnon Dou (Cave of the black spring) South Wales, UK © G.S.F Picture Library, Wye, Kent; p31 The Hood graphics © Simon Crerar/ The Sunday Times, London, 2002; p71 film still from *The Fast and the Furious* © The Ronald Grant Archive.

Copyright Artworks:
Pat Murray: ppxii–xiv, 1, 3, 13, 16–17, 22–23, 26, 34, 35–36, 41, 43, 48, 51, 53, 55, 59–60, 63, 66, 72.
Dave Hancock: pp2, 25, 44, 65.

**Every effort has been made to trace copyright holders of material reproduced in this book. Any rights not acknowledged will be acknowledged in subsequent printings if notice is given to the publisher.**

Orders: please contact Bookpoint Ltd, 130 Milton Park, Abingdon, Oxon OX14 4SB. Telephone: (44) 01235 827720, Fax: (44) 01235 400454. Lines are open from 9.00–6.00, Monday to Saturday, with a 24 hour message answering service. Email address: orders@bookpoint.co.uk

*British Library Cataloguing in Publication Data*
A catalogue record for this title is available from The British Library

ISBN 0 340 84519 8

First published 2002
Impression number   10 9 8 7 6 5 4 3 2 1
Year                            2008  2007  2006  2005  2004  2003  2002

Copyright © 2002 Kevin Eames, Karyn Taylor, David Trelawny-Ross

All rights reserved. No part of this publication may be reproduced or transmitted in any form or by any means, electronic or mechanical, including photocopy, recording, or any information storage and retrieval system, without permission in writing from the publisher or under licence from the Copyright Licensing Agency Limited. Further details of such licences (for reprographic reproduction) may be obtained from the Copyright Licensing Agency Limited, of 90 Tottenham Court Road, London W1P 9HE.

Cover photo from Michael Stones.
Typeset by Fakenham Photosetting Limited, Fakenham, Norfolk.
Printed in Great Britain for Hodder & Stoughton Educational, a division of Hodder Headline Plc, 338 Euston Road, London NW1 3BH by J.W. Arrowsmiths, Bristol.

# CONTENTS

Teachers' Introduction — v

Students' Introduction — ix

**Unit One:** Writing to imagine, explore, entertain — 1

**Unit Two:** Writing to inform, explain, describe — 23

**Unit Three:** Writing to persuade, argue, advise — 43

**Unit Four:** Writing to analyse, review, comment — 63

# Teachers' Introduction

*This book:*

1. places continual emphasis on letting students know exactly what they need to do for success at a particular level

2. breaks down success into bite-size achievable targets, particularly relevant to the learning needs of boys

3. covers all the different text-types in the Key Stage 3 Literacy Framework

4. focuses on sentence level work, to improve students' control over sentence construction

5. draws on approaches to writing embodied in the Key Stage 3 Literacy Strategy and the Progress Units

6. is designed to be used either with specific ability groups, in a mixed ability class, or with different year groups

7. aims to keep the writing process real.

*This book:*

1. places continual emphasis on letting students know exactly what they need to do for success at a particular level

**Writing: Steps to Success** is intended to help students who are currently working at a specified level to improve their writing skills so that they are able, independently, to write at a higher level. It aims to do this by giving students a detailed awareness of what writing at their target level looks like, and by making sure they are clear about what exactly they need to do to write at that level. Each book begins with a detailed comparison of two pieces of writing by students, one at the lower and the other at the upper level. Accompanying the texts is a thorough commentary, making very explicit the distinct features that differentiate the two texts from each other. The aim is to help students to be very clear about the skills they need to develop to progress from the lower to the upper level, or to consolidate and broaden their achievement if they are already beginning to write at the upper level.

### 2 breaks down success into bite-size achievable targets, particularly relevant to the learning needs of boys

Each book breaks down the skills needed to write at each level into a set of small achievable targets. As is now generally recognised, boys in particular benefit from having it made very clear to them what exactly they need to do, in small steps, to make progress. Each unit, therefore, breaks down the task of writing a particular text-type into the separate skills, mastery of which is needed to write at the level the student is working towards. In addition, each book builds on the skills learnt in the previous book. There is, therefore, a clear progression in the skills being taught so that students grow in the confidence and complexity with which they are able to demonstrate the skills essential for successful writing. Each book also focuses on the objectives of one year: **Writing: Steps to Success Level 4 to 5+** uses the Framework Objectives for Year 8 as a starting point. Together, therefore, the three books provide a chronological progression as well as a skills progression.

### 3 covers all the different text-types in the Key Stage 3 Literacy Framework

In organisation, **Writing: Steps to Success** is very simple and clear. At the beginning of each book is a Students' Introduction, with examples of students' work at the lower and upper levels relevant to that book. Through a discussion of these, students are able to form a clear picture of the differences in writing at the two levels, and to begin establishing their own targets for the skills they need to improve their own writing. Each book then has four units, each unit guiding students through the production of a piece of writing in each of the text-type triplets described in the Key Stage 3 Literacy Framework and National Curriculum 2000 document. In doing this, it ensures that the main text and sentence level objectives in the Literacy Framework for Key Stage 3 Writing are covered.

### 4 focuses on sentence level work, to improve students' control over sentence construction

The books do not aim to cover all the text and sentence level objectives. However, there is a continual emphasis on improving students' ability to control and extend their sentences, this being essential to success at a higher level. As a result, within each unit, there is a significant emphasis on developing their sentence level skills and all the sentence level objectives that are important in moving students from one level to the next are covered.

**5  draws on approaches to writing embodied in the Key Stage 3 Literacy Strategy and the Progress Units**

**Writing: Steps to Success** draws on the established best practice of English teachers and on the model of teaching writing provided by the Key Stage 3 Literacy Strategy. All units follow a similar structure. Each unit begins with a description of the particular type of writing. It then establishes the features of the type of writing, in particular, the features of that type of writing at the level relevant to that book. Students have to assess their own skills in this type of writing and, through self-assessment, set themselves the targets that they need to reach to improve their writing from one level to the next. The description and self-assessment are followed by a series of activities which guide students through the planning and writing of a text. In each unit there is a set of activities clearly focused on developing the discrete skills necessary to write successfully at the target level, with emphasis on how to improve the complexity of their sentence writing. Throughout, students are encouraged to check their work to ensure that they have met the specific criteria for success. Each unit ends with further opportunities for students to write texts of that type. These opportunities are intended to move students from being dependent on the scaffolding provided by the book and their teacher, to being independent writers, with the requisite skills for successful writing internalised.

**6  is designed to be used either with specific ability groups, in a mixed ability class, or with different year groups**

The three books are not designed to be a replacement to existing schemes of work, but as a supplementary resource. If, as part of a scheme of work, a teacher wants to develop his or her students' expertise in a particular type of writing, the books provide detailed advice on how students can achieve such expertise. The books are not intended in any way to replace the teacher. Even though the activities are written with the students as the audience and are intended to help students develop skills independently, the role of the teacher is seen as essential, in leading students through the process, and in providing opportunities to reinforce or clarify where necessary. The expertise of the teacher, therefore, is indispensable in deciding on pace, timing, groupings, and so on. It is assumed, also, that teachers will need to remind pupils of terminology, for example, clause, connective. Even at Level 3 to 4$^+$, a growing familiarity with linguistic terms, and confidence in using and applying them, will enhance the capacity of students to develop independence as writers. It is not assumed, though, that the simple recitation of terms is of value; at all times, the identification of linguistic features should be related to their effect on meaning.

Obviously, each book is particularly focused on the needs of students at one level who need to move up to the next. However, the skills taught and practised in each unit will be relevant to a far wider group than just students at the lower level of each book. A student who has attained a certain level according to their test results may well still need to learn further key skills, in order to work confidently and consistently at the level identified. The activities, therefore, provide opportunities for students to achieve a more thorough grasp of the skills necessary for success at a particular level, or for them to consolidate skills only tentatively grasped. As a result, the books do not need to be restricted to a group where all students are at the target level.

There are probably three main ways in which the books can be used. In a mixed ability class, all three books could be used concurrently, with groups of different attainment using the book relevant to their level. In a setted environment, the book most relevant to the attainment of that group could be used. Alternatively, since each book uses the Framework Objectives for one of the years at Key Stage 3 as a starting point, a different book could be used with each of Years 7 to 9.

### 7 aims to keep the writing process real

While the books embody the belief that students need to be very clear about the criteria necessary for success, the authors are aware that writing should not become simply a menu of skills to be ticked off. Equally, with the demands of writing in such a wide range of types, there is the danger that the process is reduced simply to the speedy production of very short pieces of writing displaying a narrow set of skills. Aware of these dangers, the authors want to emphasise that each unit provides opportunities to produce a substantial text, with the process marked by the familiar stages of the writing journey, and its concern to shape meaning clearly and appropriately. Accordingly, students will plan, draft, check, redraft, and reflect, as they seek to produce writing that is lively and imaginative, committed and engaging.

Ultimately, the aim is to let students in on the secret of how to write effectively in a variety of text-types, and in so doing to give them more power and more control over what they do, thus guiding them on the road to being real and successful writers.

# Students' Introduction

## How can I improve my writing from Level 4 to Level 5⁺?

To continue to improve your writing you need to know the features of writing at different levels. What are the features of writing at Level 4? How can you improve your work to reach Level 5⁺? These pages will help you to focus on some of the differences in attainment and will give you an idea of what features to target in your own work.

Read the two pieces below, and on the next page. The writers had read an article about the Loch Ness Monster, written for an American travel magazine. They were then asked to carry out this task under test conditions:

*Write an article for a travel magazine, describing a place that is beautiful but mysterious.*

*In your writing you could:*
- *try to create the atmosphere of the place in your description*
- *aim to persuade readers that this place would be an interesting place to visit.*

## Text One

Wales is a very beautiful place there is lots to do here, if you like walking there are plenty of nice walks for you. There is one place in Wales that I have been to many times it is called Shell island it is full of mystery and excitement. Its about sleeping in a tent. The road to get to Shell island gets cut off when the tide comes in but you can go fishing, crabbing, and even go in a dinghy on the water. There are plenty of rock pools to go crabbing in and just a bit further round there are beautiful sandy beaches and clear water plus a Harbour. If you are lucky you might even get a glimpse of dolphins in the water. These are the places you can visit that are within 20 miles: Dolgellau, Lanberr, Harlech, Porthmadog, Llanelli, Barmouth, Aberystwyth. On the island there are clubs, shops, gift shops, telephones and a camping shop. Plenty of room to play games: e.g. football, tennis, even baseball or rounders. It is very nice in summer. There is a fresh water lake about one and a half miles away. Plenty of places you can rent bikes from and see the sights. Plenty of restaurants and welsh chip shops. It's about 130 miles away from Lancashire. It takes about 3 hours to get there. There is also Bala lake on the way so you can stop and have something to eat. There are plenty of really nice views in wales. You can also visit the slate mines, gold mines and reservoirs. There is one where it takes you into the mountain. It is a very nice place to visit.

## Text Two

### Kitley Caves

Kitley Caves are the most beautiful and mysterious caves in the South of England. They are located in the country-side of South Devon, in an amazing wood. Just by the caves runs a river which adds to the mystery of the caves, by having a tumbling water sound through the caves. The walk to the caves is beautiful and is through a large wood and along a river. Many visitors come to the area just to stroll in the surrounding woodland area.

The actual Kitley Caves are extremely large and have many beauties inside. There are three caves you can enter and all are enormous. As well as the three caves, there are also many other caves you can look at. Inside the caves there are many geological wonders like stalagmites and stalactites, which have been formed through the slow process of dripping water. The caves are all fully lighted, creating a mysterious lighting effect inside the caves. Throughout the caves there are also many information boards describing some of the human excavations and also fossils found there. The National Trust*, who fund the caves, have placed replicas of animals whose fossils have been found. This means often you can find a hyena model sitting in the cave.

As well as the caves there is also a small museum which has exhibits found throughout the caves and a list of animals found in the 15 caves excavated. Often you can discover parties of excavators, opening a new-found cave. Some caves are 500 feet deep and have been excavated.

* Please note that the National Trust does not fund the Kitley Caves. They are under the control of Kitley Estate, Yealmpton, and the caves are no longer open to the public.

Shell Island harbour

Cave in South Wales with stalactites and stalagmites

# Discussion of the texts

These pieces were both written under test conditions. There are, of course, many things that the writers would have redrafted if they had had the time during their tests. However, Text One was graded as Level 4 and Text Two was given a Level 5. With a partner, discuss the questions below. They will also suggest ways of improving both pieces of work.

Think about the task that was set. Discuss with your partner what the writers were being asked to do.
- Think about the **form** of writing asked for. Does either piece look or sound like an article for a travel magazine?
- Think also about the **purpose** of the writing. This task asked for a **description**. Do you feel that the writers have described their chosen places effectively? The question prompts suggested that the writers could **create the atmosphere of the place**. Has either of them managed to do this? The prompts also suggested that the writers could **persuade** readers that this would be an interesting place to visit. Do you feel that the writers have persuaded you to visit their places? If so, how have they managed to do this?
- Think about the **audience** for the writing. Have these writers got a clear picture of who they are writing for? Does the writing feel as though it belongs in a travel magazine?
- How far are these two writers doing what the task asked for? Look for words and phrases that give you clues.

Now look in more detail at sentence level.
- Do these writers use **full stops** and **capital letters** accurately? All the time, or some of the time?
- What about **commas**? Do they use commas to separate items in a **list**? To mark off **phrases** and **clauses** in a sentence? All the time, or some of the time? Do they use both **single commas** and **sets of commas**, where appropriate?
- Are other forms of **punctuation** used accurately?
- Does each writer change the **tense** of verbs without a good reason?
- When they write sentences with more than one clause, do they vary their sentences with **subordinate clauses**, **co-ordinate clauses**, or a **mixture** of the two?
- Do they write both long and short sentences, for **variety**?
- Do they vary the way in which they **structure their sentences**, so that they do not always start sentences with a noun, pronoun or noun phrase?
- If they use **paragraphs**, does the first sentence of each paragraph give an idea of the topic? Do the other sentences in the paragraph develop the **topic sentence** by **explaining** in more detail or by giving detailed **examples**?
- Do the writers link sentences and paragraphs with **connectives** to signpost the reader through the text?

## What did you spot?

Now compare what you and your partner noticed with the points below. Look first at whole-text level:

- Probably the most important way to improve your writing level is to think carefully about the task set in a test or by your teacher. Think about the **form** of writing asked for. In these examples, the writers were asked for an article for a travel magazine. Both writers are enthusiastic about their chosen places, and both try to convey this to the reader, but Text One in particular does not really look or sound as though it belongs in a travel magazine, mainly because of the weaknesses in structure and organisation.
- The **purpose** of the writing is important. The writers were asked to **describe** a place that is beautiful and mysterious. Text One attempts to describe the beauty of Shell Island, but the effect of this is limited because of a repetition of *nice*. There are also several lists of places to visit and things to do, however without any real development of ideas about any one of these. For example, there is a very effective sentence: *If you are lucky you may even get a glimpse of dolphins . . .* but the writer fails to add any further detail at this point. Text Two describes the caves in more detail, attempting to describe features of their beauty. The effective vocabulary choices, such as *geological wonders, amazing wood, excavations* and *replicas of animals*, help to sustain the readers' interest and enable us to visualise what the caves may look like.
- The writers have some awareness of **audience** but this is limited. Text One seems to start off by talking to the reader, using the personal pronoun *you*, however this is unfortunately not sustained. Text Two uses a more appropriate style and content, however again there is no developed sense of a reader being addressed or persuaded.
- Overall, Text Two follows the **instructions** in the task quite closely, whereas Text One only does so in a very general way. Text Two tries to focus on both the mystery and the beauty of the caves, using both these nouns in the description given. Both writers could have tried more directly to persuade the reader that their place would be interesting to visit; this would have helped to demonstrate their awareness of the reader.

Look now in more detail at sentence level features:
- Both writers can use **full stops** and **capital letters** accurately but they don't get them right all the time. This is particularly true of Text One, where the ideas seem to come tumbling out and as a result sentences are not always clearly marked. Accurate full stops and capital letters are essential for a sound Level 4 and all levels above.
- Text One has several examples of **single commas** used correctly in **lists**. Text Two uses a **single comma** to mark off words and phrases from the rest of the sentence. For example: *They are located in the country-side of South Devon, in an amazing wood.* and *The caves are all fully lighted, creating a mysterious lighting effect inside the caves.* Text Two also uses a **single comma** to separate a subordinate clause from the main clause: *As well as the three caves, there are also many other caves you can look at.* Text Two also uses **commas in a pair**, to separate a clause in the middle of a sentence: *The National Trust, who fund the caves, have placed replicas of animals whose fossils have been found.* For a sound Level 5⁺, you need to show clearly that you understand how to use commas accurately as commas help a reader follow what you are saying more easily.

- The writer of Text One uses a colon effectively to introduce a list of ideas. Neither writer uses a wide **range of punctuation**; both writers, particularly the more confident writer of Text Two, should aim to use a variety of punctuation more regularly to support meaning.
- Both writers keep to the **present tense** and don't change it without reason. For a sound Level 4 and above, you need to know the effect of verb tenses and when you use each tense.
- Text One and Text Two both use some **co-ordinate clauses**, starting with *and* or *but*. Text One also uses a few **subordinators** like *if* and *so*. The writer of Text Two uses a wider range of **subordinators**, such as *who*, *whose* and *which*. Both writers need to use a wider range of **subordinate clauses** to improve their sentence structure. These clauses help writers to say more, giving the reader more detail about their ideas.

- Neither writer varies the **length** of sentences. Even the writer of Text Two writes a series of long sentences. Shorter sentences would be useful to emphasise points, or to make points clear.
- There is much more variety of **sentence structure** in Text Two than in Text One. Text One has a repetitive sentence structure. The writer starts most sentences with a noun (for example, *Wales*), a pronoun (*it, these*), a noun phrase (*the road, plenty of places*) or an adverb (*there*). Text Two, on the other hand, uses more interesting sentence starters. These include prepositional phrases, such as *Inside the caves* and *Throughout the caves*, as well as connectives and adverbials such as *Often, As well as,* and *This means*. These all add variety and interest to the text. Additionally, this writer uses a wide range of nouns: *caves, woods, National Trust*. This means that even though many sentences do start with the noun or noun phrase, there isn't too much repetition.
- Text One has no **paragraphs**, although the writer seems to have planned the text as ideas have been grouped together. Text Two is more helpful to the reader: it organises points in **paragraphs**. Each paragraph begins with a **topic sentence** and then develops the **topic sentence** by **explaining** in more detail or by giving detailed **examples**.
- Text One doesn't help the reader with **connectives** to link ideas. Text Two uses some connectives, such as *This means, As well as,* and *Throughout*. This helps to link points made for the reader and adds to the organisation of the text. A good **range of connectives** is needed for a sound Level 4 and above.

## Make a checklist

After you have discussed in detail the differences between these two texts, work with a partner to make a 'Level 5+ Checklist'. What things do you need to remember when you are trying to raise your writing from Level 4 to Level 5+? Make a list covering whole-text features and sentence features.

Note that your checklist will be a general one, giving an overall idea of what you need to aim at for Level 5+. In the units that follow, you will:

- look in detail at a range of writing types
- think about the features of each type of writing
- check your own writing against the features which you need to use
- track your improvements in the course of the unit.

Bear in mind that the examples which you have seen so far were written under test conditions. While you, too, will have to write under test conditions, most of your work at Key Stage 3 will be drafted. You can therefore develop ideas in detail, and work on getting punctuation correct. Aim, too, to regularly review and edit your writing, consciously focusing on trying to apply some of the techniques that you learn about. For example, most students who are aiming for Level 5+ need to vary their sentence structure and sentence length, to add to the impact of their writing. This book does not deal with spelling, but you must take care to check your spelling. You should also learn the spelling patterns which you know you find difficult. This will help you to achieve a sound Level 5+ in your writing.

Above all, keep checking. Each unit which follows will help you make a checklist of the writing features covered. If you have a checklist in your mind of the features which you should be including, you will be in control of what you are doing. And if you are in control, you will succeed. We wish you success with this process.

# Unit One

## *Writing to imagine, explore, entertain*

**In this unit, you will:**

- **think about what is special about writing to imagine, explore, entertain**
- **review your own writing, to see what needs to be done to make it a sound Level 5+**
- **look at how a professional author writes to imagine, explore, entertain**
- **draft your own writing in this form.**

Main National Framework Objectives Covered: 8Sn1, 8Sn2, 8Wr5, 8Wr7

## Writing to imagine, explore, entertain – what is it?

This kind of writing describes an experience or an event, a person or a place. It might be about something that really happened, or it might be something made up by the writer. This kind of writing makes the reader imagine something, picture something, or feel something. If the writing describes an exciting event, it should make the reader imagine that they are there. If the writing describes a person, it should make the reader feel that they can see that person, and know what they are like.

- The writer should help the reader **imagine** what someone else's experience is like, or what a place is like.
- The writer should help the reader **explore** the thoughts and feelings of the characters in the writing.
- The reader should feel **entertained** and gripped by the writing, wanting to find out what happens to the people they are reading about.

Which of the following text-types do you think are meant to imagine, explore and entertain?

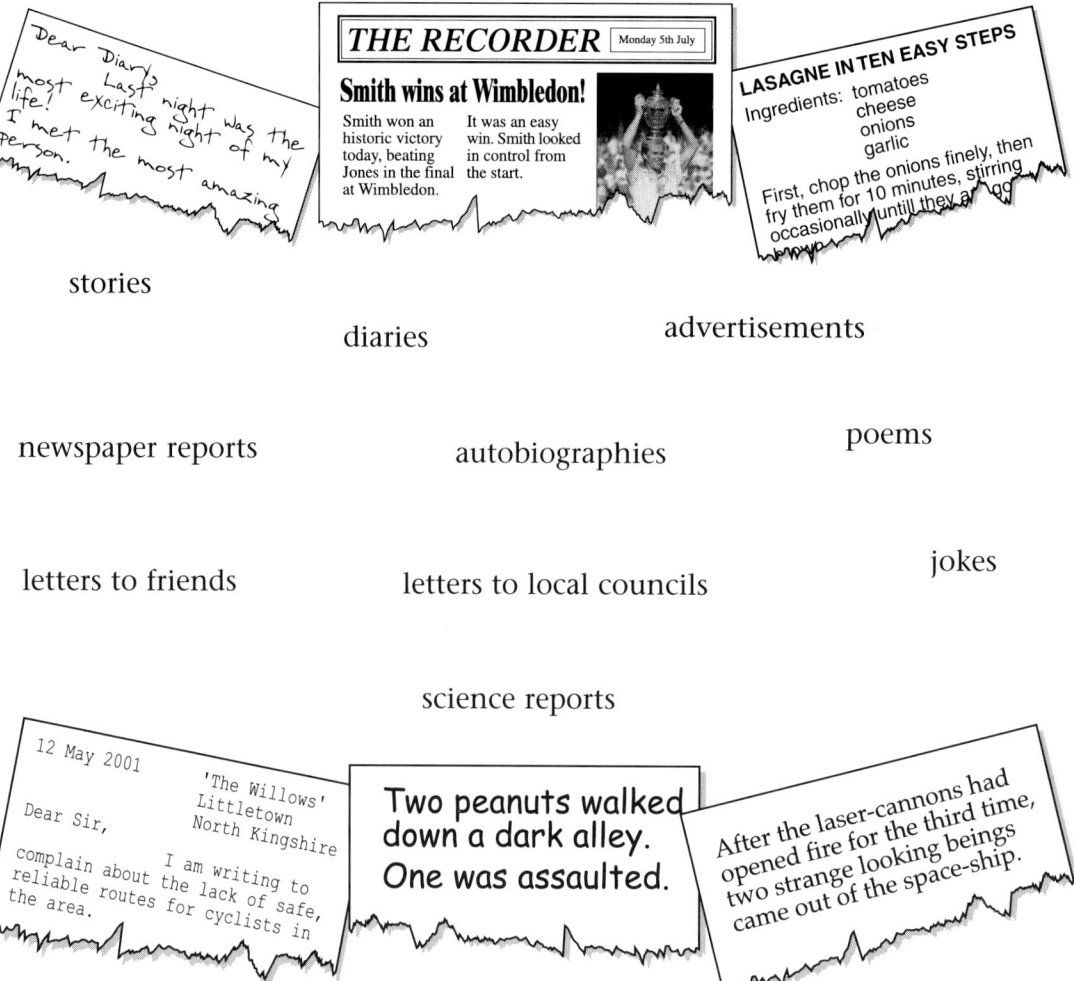

stories

diaries

advertisements

newspaper reports

autobiographies

poems

letters to friends

letters to local councils

jokes

science reports

Can you think of any other kinds of writing that are meant to imagine, explore and entertain?

# What makes a good piece of writing to imagine, explore, entertain?

So how can you be successful as a writer, in helping your reader to picture what you describe, or in grabbing and holding their attention?

Here are some of the **features** of writing to imagine, explore and entertain.

In groups, put the following features in rank order. Which are the most important features in making a piece of writing successful? Why is each important? How will it help the reader?

- an opening that makes the reader ask questions and want to read on
- interesting characters that change and surprise us
- detailed descriptions, involving all the senses
- lots of action, described in an exciting way
- dialogue that helps us understand characters
- suspense, when we wonder how problems will be solved
- variety in the sentence structure
- accurate spelling, punctuation and paragraphing.

Compare your list with the lists made by other people. Do other groups agree with your rank order? Why? Work with your teacher to make a whole-class rank order, with reasons, of the features which a successful piece of writing to imagine, explore and entertain should have. Write your final list, with the reasons, into your notebook.

# How can you improve your own writing?

Collect two or three pieces of your own writing to imagine, explore and entertain. Compare them with Text One and Text Two. Talk to your partner about the things you can do already. What things do you need to improve?

On this and the following page, there are grids which show in detail the things you need to do for a sound Level 5+. There are a lot of things to think about, but don't worry. A lot of them you will already be good at, but some you will need to improve. The grids will help you think about them. When you have finished, you will have a clear sense of what you need to improve to get a Level 5+.

Copy the grids into your notebook. (It may also be possible for your teacher to photocopy them.) For each feature, put a tick in the box which applies to you. When you have finished, you will be able to see what aspects of your work you need to focus on in the rest of this unit. You will then be able to track your targets and improvements as you write.

| FEATURES OF WRITING | I can do this sometimes | I can usually do this | I need to improve this |
|---|---|---|---|
| I start my writing in a way that gets the reader to ask questions. | | | |
| I give the reader clues suggesting problems or complications that might be developed later. | | | |
| I can write as the narrator with a clear character. | | | |
| I give details about other characters' thoughts and feelings. | | | |
| I blend together action, description, speech, thoughts and feelings to hold the reader's attention. | | | |
| In dialogue, I include gestures and actions to show the character's 'inner life'. | | | |
| I lay out dialogue accurately. | | | |
| I use adverbial phrases to give more detail about how or where actions are taking place. | | | |

| FEATURES OF WRITING | I can do this sometimes | I can usually do this | I need to improve this |
|---|---|---|---|
| I use adjectival phrases to describe people's actions, thoughts and feelings in detail. | | | |
| I confidently use a wide range of connectives to make my sentences more complex and interesting. | | | |
| I choose vocabulary precisely for effect. | | | |
| I separate words, phrases and clauses in sentences with a single comma. | | | |
| I separate words, phrases and clauses in sentences with a pair of commas. | | | |
| I choose when to separate a subordinate clause from a main clause with a comma. | | | |
| I end sentences with a full stop. | | | |
| I start sentences with a capital letter. | | | |
| I use short sentences for effect. | | | |
| I write longer sentences for description. | | | |
| I start a new paragraph when I change topic or time. | | | |
| I check my drafts carefully for the spellings and patterns I have trouble with. | | | |

 Now that you have reviewed your writing, record in your notebook the main things that you need to work on and improve. Keep checking your progress throughout the unit.

# Getting started: finding ideas to write about

Your story will be in three main sections: the opening, the complication, and the ending or resolution. Before we look in detail at how to write your story, you need to find ideas to write about. You need to have some ideas about the whole story.

## Planning your story

Here are two examples of story beginnings. With at least one other person, discuss for each beginning what might happen next, and how each story might end.

*You are a young man about to start your first job. Another man who works at the same company tells you he needs your help with something. It sounds suspicious but since you are new, you decide to go along with him.*

*You are a teenage girl. Your mother asks you to collect your little sister on the way home from school. On your way you meet someone. Who is it? What do they say? What happens then?*

Now plan your ideas for your own story by answering the following questions. Think-write your ideas in your notebook and remember you can change them later if you choose.

- You are going to write in the **first person**, as the **narrator** of your story (more about that later in the unit). Therefore you need to make a few choices about who you are. What age and sex will you be? A young man? A teenage girl? An old woman?
- You will need to introduce a second character. What age and sex will they be? Will you know them or will they be a stranger?
- You will need to decide on a complication. For example, someone might dare you to do something, an accident might happen or you might stumble on a crime being committed.
- You need to decide how you deal with the problem. What happens? How does it end?

## The opening of your writing

The opening of your story is obviously very important, because you want to hook the reader in so that they want to keep on reading.

When you write your opening, you will be learning how to:

- write as a narrator with a clear character
- make the reader want to ask questions about what is about to happen.

Here is the beginning of the novel *Daz 4 Zoe*, by Robert Swindells. The novel is set in the future when the rich and poor are kept apart and live totally different lives. Subbies and Chippies are the names they give to the rich and the poor. Daz is a Chippy from the poor side of the city and Zoe is a Subby from the rich side.

Read the opening paragraphs on page 7 and then discuss these questions with a partner:

- What did you notice straight away about the opening?
- How are the two narrators different in the way that they speak?

*Writing to imagine, explore, entertain*

- What sort of people do the two narrators sound like?
- What information did you learn about the two narrators?
- What questions does the opening make you ask about what has happened or what might be about to happen?

## Daz

*Daz thay call me. 2 years back wen I com 13 Del that's my brovver <u>thay catch im raiding wiv the Dred. Top im</u> don't thay, and im just gon 15.*

*2 lornorders com tel our mam, 1 wumin, 1 man, nor thay don't come til after thay dunnit neever. Our Mam been down a longtime fore then wiv the dulleye, and <u>she just sort of stairs dont she</u>, til thay go of, and its not til nite she crys.*

*She sez dont you never go of wiv no Dred, our Daz. No Mam, I sez, but <u>I never crost my hart. Don't cownt less you crost yor hart, rite?</u>*

> written to sound as if he's talking with a strong accent

> written to sound like he's talking to the reader

> hints at what he might do later in the story

## Zoe

*<u>Hi</u>. I'm Zoe. Zoe May Askew. Or Zoe may not. (Joke!) I'm fourteen. My friend at school is Tabitha. Tabitha Flinders Wentworth for short. She's fourteen too. If the name seems familiar <u>to you</u> it's no big surprise. Her dad's Paul Wentworth of Wentworth and Lodge (Developments) PLC, the outfit that shoved up practically every residential estate in practically every suburb in England. You're bound to have seen their boards, plus their ads on T.V. He's into about a million other things too, Tabby says. Security. Roads. Power. He's into power all right.*

*They're loaded. Well, you can imagine. They live in this gorgeous architect-designed house on Wentworth Drive. That's right – Wentworth Drive. He built the place and named it after himself, and why not?*

*Listen. I want to tell you a story, only I've got to start at the beginning, right? And that's where Tabby Wentworth comes in. At the beginning. Because she <u>started it</u>. She started it because everything's boring and fourteen's a lousy age and chippying's about the only way you can get a bit of excitement around here. Chippying. If you've never heard of it, don't worry. You will. In fact you're going to know all about chippying real soon.*

> chatty, informal style, but matter-of-fact, not over-dramatic

> uses second-person pronoun to talk directly to the reader

> hints at what will happen to make us read on

7

# It's your turn

## Planning your opening

Before you start writing the opening, you need to make some choices about what you are going to put in to the opening of your story.

You are writing this story in the first person, as the narrator. That means it sounds as if you are telling the story, using *I did this* ... and *I felt* ... You have already begun to think about who you will be as the narrator. Now make some choices about what sort of person you will be. Rough? Hard? Thoughtful? Sensitive? Will you be positive and friendly or angry and suspicious? How will you speak? In an accent or in standard English? Will you speak straight to the reader, using the second-person pronoun *you*, as Zoe does?

What will you tell the reader about yourself? What physical details will you give?

Get a picture in your head of where you want to start your story. In a house? In a park? On a street? What will the weather be like?

What description will you use? Try to include all the senses.

In your journal, brainstorm your ideas about what you see, hear, feel, think.

You also need to think about what hints or clues you will give the reader that something exciting or scary or awful is going to happen later in the story. In the extract, Zoe says:

*Chipping. If you've never heard of it, don't worry. You will. In fact you're going to know all about chippying real soon.*

What hints does that give us about what will happen?

## Writing your opening

Here's a brainstorm for an opening:

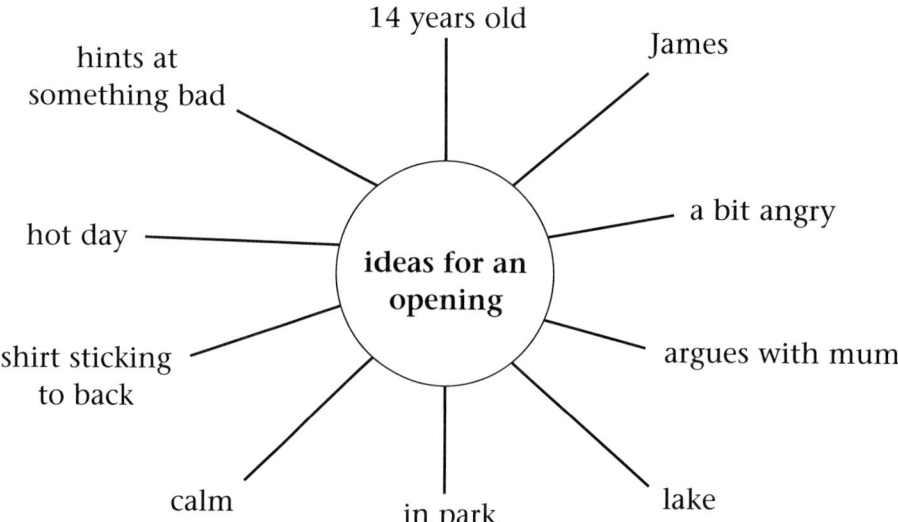

This is how it came out as an opening:

*My name's James. I'm fourteen. You probably think I'm like any other teenager. Always angry, always ready for an argument. Well, I was, but I'm not now, not after it happened.*

*It was a hot day. It was so hot I remember feeling my shirt sticking to my back. I had had a row with my mum. You're probably wondering what's unusual about that. Teenagers are meant to have rows with their mum. You're right: we often had rows, but not like that. Maybe that's why I went to the park. It's odd to think that if I hadn't had a row, I wouldn't have gone to the park and then, well, it would all be different wouldn't it?*

*The park is where I go to cool down. Maybe you've got a place like that. Somewhere where you can't be found, where you can think and be on your own. So, there's a lake and trees and . . .*

Notice how the writer has:
- begun with short sentences to make the narrator sound like he is just trying to get the facts across, and can't really be bothered to explain everything in detail
- hinted at the rest of the story by saying *it*, but not explained what *it* is and by saying that it changed him, but without saying how or why
- used the second-person pronoun *you* to make it sound like he is talking to the reader.

Now have a go at writing your opening. It should be longer than this one, about 300 words, but don't get carried away and tell the whole story! Remember you don't have to use all the ideas from your brainstorm. Before you start you could underline your best ideas. Try to hint at what will happen later and how it will affect you, to make the reader want to ask questions.

**Checking your work**
Read your work with a partner and answer these questions.

- What have you told the reader about yourself as narrator?
- What tone of voice does the narrator have?
- Have you included the second-person pronoun *you*?
- Have you included description of sounds, sights, smells?
- What hints have you written about what will happen, or how it will affect you?
- Are there any words spelt wrongly?

**Writing: Steps to Success** *Level 4 to 5+*

## Writing the next section: using dialogue

In this section, you will introduce another character and use dialogue or conversation to lead the reader toward the complication, which will be the most exciting part of your story. One of the things you need to be able to do to get a Level 5+ is to write good dialogue or conversation. In this section, you will be learning about how to write dialogue with:

- correct layout and punctuation
- thoughtful choice of verbs
- thoughtful choice of other description to add detail and atmosphere.

As an example of interesting dialogue, here is another extract from *Daz 4 Zoe*. You met the two characters earlier. You will remember that Daz is a Chippy from the poor side of the city and Zoe is a Subby from the rich side. Breaking all the rules, Daz and Zoe have met and fallen in love. In this extract they are meeting for the second time. If they are caught the consequences would be disastrous, since Subbies and Chippies are forbidden from having any kind of relationship with each other. Dred is the name of a terrorist organisation that kills the rich Subbies.

'D'you go to school?' I asked. I knew Chippies don't have to go, some do, some don't. He told me he got thrown out and when I asked why he grinned and said, 'Fooling around – thinking about you when I should've been thinking about my lessons.'

<u>I nodded</u>. 'I got in trouble for that too, but chucked out – that's a bit rough, surely?'

<u>He shrugged</u>. 'Big city. One school. Plenty kids waiting to go. I was gonna quit anyway.'

'What for? I mean, what d'you do now?'

'Nothing. I wanted to join Dred, only they turned me down.'

'You wanted –.' I looked at him. 'Why'd you want to be a in a terrorist organisation, for pete's sake?' <u>I realised I knew pitifully little about him.</u>

'Why?' He looked down, hacking the dirt with the heel of his trainer. 'They topped our Del for a kickoff. And I hate Subbies.'

'I'm a Subby.' Yes, I told myself. And here I am sitting in the dark with the guy. How do I know he's not fixing to cut my throat? <u>I wasn't scared, though. I couldn't believe he'd hurt me. It was unthinkable.</u>

'Yeah.' <u>He loosened a small stone and flicked it away with his toe.</u> 'I know. That's how come they knocked me back.'

'How d'you mean?'

*[annotations: gesture and body language to show feeling; character's thoughts; action to hint at character's thoughts]*

**Writing to imagine, explore, entertain**

> [new line for new speaker] 'They saw us. You and me. At the club. They've got me figured for a Subby-lover.'
> I nodded. 'My so-called friends've taken to calling me Chippy-lover.'
> 'Why?' He <u>gripped my hands so tight it hurt</u>. 'Do they know about me?' [action to hint at character's feelings and thoughts]
> 'No.' I tried to free my hands. He realised what he was doing and relaxed his grip, but he seemed about to jump up and run.
> 'No, they don't know about you. How could they? I didn't know about you myself till tonight, did I? And if I had, d'you think I'd have told anyone? I'm not a fool, Daz.'
> [varied choice of verbs] He <u>chuckled</u>, shaking his head. 'Okay, Zoe. I'm jumpy, right? They find me here, I die. For a minute I thought –.'
> 'Listen.' I looked in his eyes. 'I think you better go soon, anyway.' He'd laughed, but his reaction had reminded me of the risk he was taking. I told him he'd better go but I didn't want him to, and so to keep him I <u>said</u>, 'Who was Del?'
> 'My brother. He was fifteen.'
> 'And they – executed him?'
> 'Topped him, yeah.'

Read the passage on pages 10 and above, and then discuss these questions with a partner.

- What facts do you learn from the passage about the two characters?
- What can you tell about how they are feeling and thinking?
- Find some evidence to back up your answers.
- Count how many verbs of speaking there are. Why do you think there are so few?
- What does the writer describe as well as giving us the actual words spoken?

 Now fill in the following table on page 12 to look in detail at the way the writer has constructed the dialogue using **body language**, the **thoughts** of the characters and **actions**. Each of these added details helps us get inside the character's head to see what they are really thinking and feeling. That makes them seem more like real people and therefore makes the conversation more interesting and believable to us as readers. For each of the details in the table try to write what you think it might show us about the character's inner life, their inside thoughts and feelings. For each you will probably need to read the conversation again, first, to see why they are behaving like that.

| Body language<br>*He shrugged.*<br>*I looked at him.* | What could it show? |
|---|---|
| Thoughts<br>*I wasn't scared, though.* | What could it show? |
| Action<br>*He gripped my hands so tight it hurt.* | What could it show? |

You can see how the writer often lets us know what the characters are thinking and feeling by telling us what they do and how they do it rather than always spelling it out.

### Using the correct layout and punctuation

Look again at the passage and answer these questions to come up with three rules for the layout and punctuation of dialogue.

- When do you start a new line?
- Where do you put speech marks?
- Do you put other punctuation, like commas and question marks, inside or outside the speech marks?

### Verbs of speaking

Although, the writer of this passage doesn't use a wide range of verbs of speaking, you should aim to have a good variety of well-chosen verbs. In pairs, see if you can think of thirty verbs? Here are five to get you started: *whisper, hiss, mumble, screech* and *stammer*.

# It's your turn

## Planning your dialogue

Look back at your plan to remind yourself who your second character is and what they say to you to lead on to the complication later in your story.

You now need to make some more detailed choices about what sort of person they are and also what you will talk about. Do another brainstorm to answer these questions:

- Where will you meet them?
- What will they be wearing?
- What will be their mood?
- Have you met them before?
- Will they be smaller or bigger, older or younger than you?
- How will meeting them make you feel? Nervous? Excited? Curious or suspicious?
- What will they tell you or ask you for?

Here is a brainstorm which could follow the beginning you read earlier.

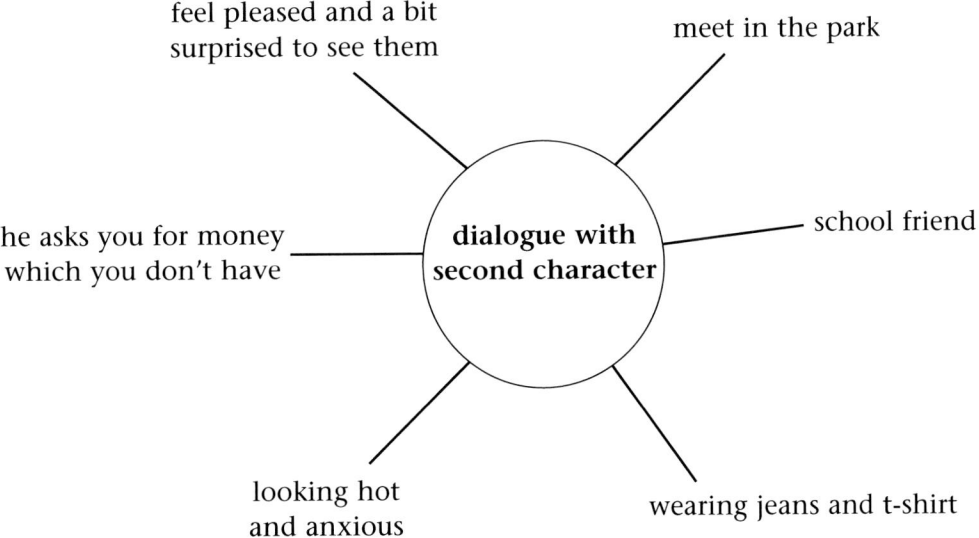

Here is how the conversation could go:

*Suddenly, I heard my name being called. I turned round and saw Steven from school. He was in my year, but taller than me. He had brown hair and blue eyes. He always looked like he'd just got out of bed.*
*'Hi there, how are you doing?' I asked, looking at him. His forehead was sweating with the heat, his chest was heaving.*
*He was out of breath with running to catch me up. 'Alright,' he wheezed between breaths, 'actually not alright, I need your help.' His eyes flicked from the ground to my eyes. He was clearly nervous.*
*There was a pause. I waited for him to say more. When he didn't I asked, 'What can I do?'*

Copy the following table and fill in examples of thoughts, body language, actions, description and interesting verbs of speaking.

| Thoughts | |
|---|---|
| Body language | |
| Actions | |
| Description | |
| Interesting verbs of speaking | |

## Writing your dialogue

Now write your conversation from the notes you have made, remembering the three rules of layout and punctuation and remembering to include the body language, actions, interesting verbs of speaking and thoughts.

### Checking your work

Read your work with a partner and then answer these questions:

- Have you described the second character to the reader?
- Have you told the reader about the problem or complication in your story?
- Is there more speaking or more description of action, thoughts and body language in your conversation?
- Count how many times you have described action, thoughts and body language.
- How many interesting verbs and adverbs have you used? Can you improve on any that you have used?
- Have you laid out the dialogue with a new line for each speaker?
- Have you included all the right punctuation?

## The complication and ending

In this final section, you will write the ending of your story. It will include the problem or crisis or disaster you have been hinting at and it will bring the story to some kind of a close.

You will be also be learning how to make your writing more interesting by the way you:
- blend action, dialogue, description together with the thoughts and feelings of the characters
- use adjectival and adverbial phrases to make your sentences more complex and to fill out the picture of what is happening
- choose vocabulary precisely for effect
- use a range of punctuation effectively, including commas and speech marks.

## Another example from *Daz 4 Zoe*

In the extract below from near the end of the book, Daz and Zoe are trying to escape from the city to a new life together. But they have been caught by the gang, Dred, who want revenge for something Daz did earlier in the book. They are in the basement of the school Daz used to go to. Cal, one of the gang, is about to shoot off Daz's kneecap, before killing him. Pohlman is a policeman, who they thought had been trying to catch them.

Read the extract below and on the following page, making sure you understand what has happened, and then with a partner discuss the questions that follow.

| Annotation | Extract | Annotation |
|---|---|---|
| sense of sound | <u>The shot, and the agonised scream</u> which followed it echoed deafeningly through the basement. <u>Sick with horror, yet driven by a compulsion I was powerless to resist</u> I turned. Daz, <u>supported by Mick and Smithy</u>, was still on his feet. Cal was kneeling on the floor with his arms wrapped round his stomach, screaming. His <u>broken</u> glasses lay in a <u>crimson</u> splotch on the floor. As I gaped, the two men let go of Daz and turned toward the stairs. <u>I turned, too.</u> Pohlman was crouching on the bottom step <u>with a smoking gun in his fist</u>. Smithy was raising his own weapon when Pohlman fired again. The gunman <u>spun</u> round and <u>crumpled</u>, his pistol <u>skittering</u> away across the cement. Mick, <u>seeing Pohlman momentarily distracted</u>, doused his torch and made a dash for it, knocking the policeman sideways and leaping on to the stairs. There was a shot, a cry and a metallic clatter. A <u>light which had been shining from somewhere behind Pohlman</u> went out and the basement was plunged into blackness. | Zoe's thoughts |
| | | adjectival phrase |
| | | adjectives to add detail |
| short sentence to stop the action – creates suspense | | adverbial phrase |
| verbs chosen to create precise image | | subordinate clause beginning with -ing word |
| subordinate clause beginning with relative pronoun | | |

| | |
|---|---|
| sense of touch | A <u>grip clamped</u> my arm, Daz yelled, <u>'Come on!'</u> and I was dragged, totally blind, across the floor. I don't know how he knew where to go, but almost at once I tripped on the first step and then we were climbing. There was a heck of a racket <u>–</u> shouting, shooting, some sort of motor. Anyway, there we were, going up into blackness <u>and</u> then I saw light <u>–</u> a glimmer and some flashes <u>and</u> we were up in the lobby <u>and</u> somebody had a spotlight on it <u>so</u> I couldn't see much more than in the dark. |

- speech inserted into action
- long sentence to make series of actions seem endless, joined with co-ordinating connectives
- dashes to make sentences move faster – adds tension

- What is the difference between what we expect to happen and what actually happens at the beginning of the first paragraph?
- What do you notice about the length of sentences in the second paragraph?
- What do you notice about which sense is described most in the second paragraph? Why is this?
- Which words give you very precise pictures of what the characters are doing or feeling?
- What is significant about the words the writer has chosen?
- What do you notice about the way the writer has varied and expanded his sentences?

# It's your turn

## Writing your ending

Your task will be to write the ending of your story in a way that uses the same features as Robert Swindells uses. As before, first brainstorm your ideas in your journal about:
- what will happen, how the problem or crisis will develop and reach a conclusion
- how it will link to the beginning and middle of the story
- the thoughts and feelings of your characters
- the different senses you can include
- how it will end; will it tie everything up or will it leave the reader asking questions?

Here is a brainstorm for an ending that could follow on from the dialogue in the last section:

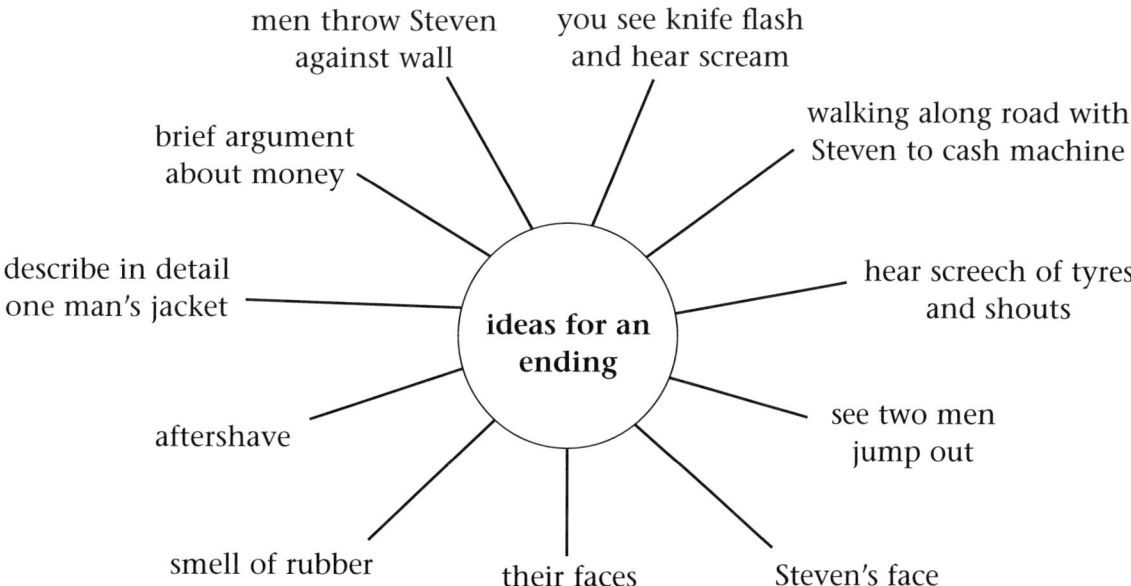

## Writing blending action, description, speech, and thoughts

Look again at the beginning of the third paragraph of the extract.

*A grip clamped my arm, Daz yelled, 'Come on!' and I was dragged, totally blind, across the floor. I don't know how he knew where to go, but almost at once I tripped on the first step and then we were climbing. There was a heck of a racket ...*

Work out which part of this extract is action, which is description of sounds or other senses, which is speech, and which is thoughts. The writer could simply have written:

*Daz dragged me up the stairs ...*

By blending together all the different elements, the writer makes a very 'three-dimensional' picture of what is going on. It helps us experience it for ourselves.

When choosing the description it is important to use the full range of senses and to pick out small details to describe in depth. For example, Swindells, in the second paragraph writes:

*His broken glasses lay in a crimson splotch on the floor.*

Notice how much information that one short sentence gives you; the glasses have fallen off, they are broken, there is blood on the floor. Include details like that which fill out our three-dimensional picture for the reader to experience every angle of the action.

Now practise writing like this yourself. Using the brainstorm on page 17 you could start with something like:

*We were walking down the High Street to the cash machine. **(action)** I could feel the sun on my neck and hear Steven's trainers slapping the pavement. **(sense of touch and sound)** 'God, it's hot', I said, **(speech)** trying to break the awkward silence. Steven said nothing, and I was beginning to wish I hadn't bothered to help him. **(thoughts)***

Now write the first four or five sentences of your ending, make sure you include action, description, thoughts and speech. When you have finished, with a partner underline what you have written in four colours, one each for action, description, thoughts and speech.

## Using a wide range of adverbial and adjectival phrases

To write for Level 4 you learnt how to use noun phrases and adverbial phrases to give extra detail to your writing. To write at Level 5+ you need to continue to do this, but you need to be more adventurous in the extra description you add and in the way you make your sentences more complex through your use of **adjectival** and **adverbial phrases**.

Look again at these sentences from the extract.

*Daz, <u>supported by Mick and Smithy</u>, was still on his feet.*
*Cal was kneeling on the floor <u>with his arms</u> wrapped round his stomach*
*Pohlman was crouching on the bottom step <u>with a smoking gun in his fist</u>.*

Each of the sentences on the previous page makes sense without the phrase underlined. However, the underlined phrase adds meaning, helping us form a much better picture of what is going on.

Each of these phrases either helps describe a person or an action. The first describes Daz and is called an **adjectival phrase**. The second and third give extra information about the actions of Cal and Pohlman and are called **adverbial phrases**. If the phrase has a verb in it, it is called a clause.
You need to include lots of phrases or clauses in your story which add information about the **character** or the **action**.

## Some points to remember about adding phrases and clauses

You can put the phrase at the beginning of the sentence, or in the middle or at the end. In this sentence, *Daz, supported by Mick and Smithy, was still on his feet*, the clause is in the middle of the sentence. In this one: *Cal was kneeling on the floor with his arms wrapped round his stomach*, it is at the end of the sentence.

If you put a clause at the beginning of the sentence you will almost always need a comma after it, before the rest of the sentence. If you put a clause into the middle of the sentence, sometimes called a 'drop-in clause', it will need a pair of commas around the clause. In the second example above, there is a pair of commas around the clause: *, supported by Mick and Smithy,* which has been 'dropped into' the sentence.

There are two good ways to start subordinate clauses. You can begin them with a word ending in -ing. For example, *Hearing the sound of his voice, I quickly turned around.* You can also begin them with a wide range of connectives, for example; *when, while, as, during, although*. For example, *When I heard the sound of his voice, I quickly turned around.* When you begin a sentence in either of these ways, remember to put a comma after the subordinate clause.

If you join two clauses together in a sentence with an *and*, an *or* or a *but*, then the clauses are called co-ordinating clauses, and you do not need a comma to separate them.

## Using vocabulary with precision for effect

The author, Robert Swindells, uses well-chosen vocabulary to create very strong pictures for the reader. In each of the following sentences, look at the word underlined and discuss with a partner what picture or image the word gives you, and then fill in the table.

He <u>stooped</u>, <u>thrusting</u> the gun into the crook of Daz's knee.
<u>Sick</u> with horror ... I turned.
Pohlman was <u>crouching</u> on the bottom step ...
The gunman spun round and <u>crumpled</u>, his pistol <u>skittering</u> away across the cement ...

| Word | Picture or feeling |
|---|---|
| thrusting | *This gives me a picture of Cal really pushing the gun into the back of his knee, not just lightly resting it there.* |
| stooped | |

Now rewrite the following passage changing the words underlined for something more precise. You might want to use a thesaurus.

*The men <u>were talking</u> to Steven. His face was <u>scared</u>. They <u>went up to</u> him and <u>put him</u> against the wall. One of them <u>held</u> his shoulders. I <u>saw</u> the other <u>put</u> his hand into his pocket and <u>take out</u> a knife. The blade <u>shone</u> in the sunshine. His arm <u>moved</u> suddenly. Steven <u>made a noise</u>.*

## Writing your own ending

After all this practising it is now time to write your own ending! First, read through your story so far. Next look again at your plan. Aim to write about five or six paragraphs and make sure you:

- include description, using all the senses, including describing interesting details in depth
- include vocabulary chosen precisely for effect
- try to start some sentences with subordinate clauses, beginning with a connective like *when, while, as, during* or a word ending in -ing
- try to add some 'drop-in' clauses into the sentences
- try to end a sentence with an adverbial phrase that adds information to the action you have described
- remember to put the commas before or after the subordinate clause where necessary.

## Revising your draft

Well done, you have now finished a first draft of your story. You will need to revise it before you write your final version. As you have written it in three sections you may need to make some changes to ensure each section flows into the next, or to make sure the plot is not too confusing. First, ask a few people to read over the whole story.

Ask them to tell you:
- What picture they had in their mind of the people and places in your story. (Did you help them **imagine** the people and places?)
- Whether your story reminded them of anything, made them think of anything, or gave them new ideas about anything. (Did you help them to **explore** thoughts, feelings or ideas?)
- What they enjoyed about your story. (Did it **entertain** them?)

Ask them also to tell you:
- What they liked about the way you wrote the story – for example, the way it made them ask questions at the beginning, the description you included, the range of short and long sentences.
- Whether they have any questions about things that aren't clear, or need explaining in more detail.
- Whether they have any ideas for improving parts of your story.

Now check your story before writing out a final copy.
- Have you ended each sentence with a **full stop**? (Work with a partner. Count the number of sentences you have written in each paragraph. Write the number in the margin. Then count the number of full stops. The numbers should be the same!)
- Do all your sentences **begin with a capital letter**? (Underline the first word of each sentence. Has it got a capital letter?)
- Have you used **capital letters for names**? (Underline each name in your story. Put a ring round the first letter. Is it a capital?)
- Have you used lots of adverbial and adjectival phrases, at the beginning, in the middle or at the end of sentences?
- Have you separated **subordinate clauses** from main clauses with **commas**? (Look at the start of each clause to see if it begins with a connective. If there is a connective, put a box around it. Where should the comma go?)
- Have you used a **range of connectives**? (Look at the connectives you have marked. If you have used more than one *and* clause in a sentence, is there a good reason? Have you used five other connectives, apart from *and* or *but*?)

And:
- Have you started a **new paragraph** when you change **topic, time** or **speaker**? (Read through your draft, and label each new paragraph as topic, time or talk. Do you need to join some paragraphs or to split others?)
- Have you checked the **punctuation of speech**? (Revise the rules. Put a ring round the speech marks that begin and end speech. Remember the comma and the capital letter. Where do they go?)

And finally:
- Check your draft carefully for the **spelling patterns** you know you have trouble with. (Use your spelling list to remind you.)

If you can answer yes to most of these questions, well done, you are almost certainly writing at Level 5+.

## And you could try ...

Here are a few extra ideas for writing to imagine, explore and entertain. You may like to try at least one of them. Use the techniques that you have been developing in this unit. Think about your individual targets for improvement, and work on them. Finally, think about presentation – not just handwriting, but whether you could use word-processing and illustrations to make your story look good.

- What about designing a cover and writing a blurb? What about getting it bound into a book?
- What about having a publisher's party, where your class brings in (not too messy!) food and drink? You could read each other's books, and write reviews, like the book reviews in newspapers and magazines. You will need to collect examples of these reviews, to see what reviewers say, and how they say it. You could make a wall display from the reviews written by your class.
- You could write about a true story. It could be something that happened to you or a friend, someone in your family, or it could be something you heard about on the news.
- You could try writing as a narrator who is very different to you, maybe someone who is a parent, an old person, someone from a different country. Try to imagine what it must be like to be them and write with the thoughts, feelings and opinions you think they would have.
- You could try different ways of opening your story. You could open it with dialogue, and then introduce the narrator later.
- Don't forget to keep thinking about making choices about the plot, about the characters, about what description to include, about what sorts of sentences and vocabulary to use.

# Unit Two

## *Writing to inform, explain, describe*

**In this unit, you will:**

- think about what is special about writing to inform, explain, describe

- review your own writing, to see what needs to be done to make it a sound Level 5+

- look at how a professional author writes a newspaper article to inform, explain, describe

- draft your own writing in this form.

Main National Framework Objectives Covered: 7Sn7, 7Sn11, 7Wr10, 7Wr11, 8Wd11, 8Sn1, 8Sn3, 8Sn6, 8Wr11, 8Wr12, 9Sn4, 9Wr12

# Writing to inform, explain, describe – what is it?

The majority of the writing you read in school (and out of school) is probably writing to **inform**, **explain** and **describe**. This writing covers a wide range of topics or subjects.

- Writing to **inform** gives you facts. It does not try to persuade you to follow one particular viewpoint or argument. For example, it may be writing you find in a Religious Studies textbook, such as *What is Buddhism?* You may find it on the Internet (e.g. when searching for information on *food suitable for hedgehogs*). You may also find it in a newspaper, for example, in an article entitled: *Ten outdoor activity summer holidays for teenagers*. It may be an advice leaflet from your doctor's surgery, about the signs and symptoms of meningitis. The writer tells us information so we may find out new facts. This writing usually answers the questions: Who? What? Where? When?

- Writing to **explain** helps to make something plain or clear to the reader. For example, the writing may be explaining why soil erosion occurs, or what happens to the food we eat. The writer is usually explaining processes or difficult ideas. Often diagrams are used to support the explanation given in the body of the text. Explanations give us many facts. There may be more than one explanation or reason for an event, though, so writers then pick the most important information for the reader. For example, if we think about why soil erosion occurs we may come up with several reasons. These reasons will form part of the explanation. Writing to explain usually answers the questions why and how.

- Writing to **describe** often combines information and explanation. The writer describes what happened during a particular time or event. For example, they could write a description of life in India during the rainy season. They could also write a description of what happened during the World Cup, including what a particular football team felt about the event. This writing may answer a range of questions (including who, what, when, where, why, or how), depending on what the writer chooses to focus on. The writer selects what details to put into their description. Of the three forms of writing, descriptive writing is most likely to include adjectives, imagery and descriptive detail. You will also find lots of examples of descriptive writing in fiction texts that you read.

There are several overlaps between these forms of writing. A leaflet about a disease such as malaria, for example, may include information about symptoms. It may also explain what to do if you think you have the disease. It may also describe different types of malaria and where they are found. This kind of writing is rarely pure information, explanation or description. It is usually a mixture of text-types, with features of all three types of writing.

# Writing to inform, explain, describe

 Discuss the following text-types. Which ones are meant to inform, explain and describe? Which ones have a combination of these types of writing? Discuss the list and see what you think.

a television programme about the possible effects of continued global warming
a story about a refugee living in a refugee camp on the border of Afghanistan
'the story of a chip: what happens once it's eaten'
a description of life in a Brazilian rain forest
an encyclopaedia entry about walruses
a leaflet entitled 'Drugs: their use and abuse'
a fantasy novel
a letter to the newspaper complaining about a new housing development
a journal entry entitled 'My trip to the North Pole – day 37'
an advertisement about a new shower gel
a science experiment
your school report
a letter about the new savings rates offered by a bank
an essay entitled 'The problems facing Zimbabwe'
a leaflet from Greenpeace about why they are protesting against mining on the beaches
an evaluation of your set design in Drama
an extract from a travel magazine about the Caribbean
an Internet site run by the 'Save the Dolphin' society
an explanation of how hot-air balloons work
a private diary entry
a science fiction story
a letter from a soldier fighting in World War One
an editorial about railway strikes
a newspaper article about how to help wild animals survive winter

# What makes a good piece of writing to inform, explain, describe?

You now have an idea about the general features of writing to inform, explain and describe. You have also discussed some examples of these types of writing. For homework, collect as many different types of these types of writing as you can. You need to use a variety of sources to try and find as many different forms of this writing as possible. You could look in the following places:
- the Internet
- an encyclopaedia
- school textbooks (remember to look at writing in other subjects, not just English)
- newspapers and magazines
- free information leaflets (available in supermarkets, Tourist Information Centres, DIY shops, pharmacies, doctors' surgeries, and so on)
- your own writing in a range of subjects.

Working in groups, look at the examples you have collected. What **features** of writing to inform, explain and describe can you identify? Use your knowledge of non-fiction text-types to help you to identify key features at word, sentence and text level. Do you think that some of the group's examples are better than others? Can you explain why? Here are some ideas to help you to focus your discussion:

- Is there a heading that makes the **purpose** of the writing clear to the reader?
- Who is the **audience** for the writing? How do you know?
- How does the writer **catch our attention**?
- Are there **sub-headings** or **diagrams** to help us? How are these features helpful to the reader?
- Is the writing clear, with effective use of **connectives** to link ideas? Collect examples of different ways in which the writers connect their ideas.
- Is the **vocabulary** varied and interesting?
- Is the writing **well-structured** with varied sentence structures and sentence length?

## How can you improve your own writing?

Collect two or three pieces of your own writing to inform, explain and describe. Remember to look at writing in other subjects, as well as in English. Compare them with the two examples in the Students' Introduction. Talk to a partner about the things you do already. What things do you need to improve?

On this and the following page, there are grids which show in detail the things you need to do to achieve a sound Level 5$^+$. There are a lot of things to think about, but don't worry. A lot of them you will already be good at, but some you will need to improve on. The grids will help you think about which areas you need to improve. If you are not sure about a feature, your teacher will be able to explain. You could also wait to see how the feature is used later in the unit.

Copy the grids into your notebook. (It may also be possible for your teacher to photocopy them.) For each feature, put a tick in the box which applies to you. When you have finished, you will be able to see what you need to focus on in the rest of this unit. You will then be able to track your targets and improvements as you write.

| FEATURES OF WRITING | I can do this sometimes | I can usually do this | I need to improve this |
|---|---|---|---|
| I capture the reader's interest with an effective heading and writing style. | | | |
| I focus on layout to make my text appealing, using diagrams, tables and illustrations, if appropriate. | | | |
| I write in a formal/impersonal or informal/personal style, as needed. | | | |
| I plan carefully and structure my writing to suit its purpose. | | | |
| I explain clearly and confidently so that the reader understands my explanation and my writing is credible. | | | |
| I include quotations in my writing and these are accurately punctuated. | | | |
| I select the amount of detail to use, for the purpose of my writing. | | | |
| I choose whether to write in a plain style or to include more detail and description for effect. | | | |

| FEATURES OF WRITING | I can do this sometimes | I can usually do this | I need to improve this |
|---|---|---|---|
| I start sentences with a capital letter and end sentences with a full stop, question mark or exclamation mark. | | | |
| I write all proper nouns with a capital letter. | | | |
| I select the correct verb tense to use and use it consistently. | | | |
| I vary the length of my sentences and write short sentences for effect. | | | |
| I start my sentences in different ways, to add variety and interest. | | | |
| I use a range of connectives to link my ideas together and to guide the reader through the text. | | | |
| I divide my ideas into paragraphs, each with a topic sentence and supporting detail. | | | |
| I vary the position of subordinate clauses to make my sentences more interesting. | | | |
| I separate words, phrases and clauses in sentences with a single comma. | | | |
| I separate words, phrases and clauses in sentences with a pair of commas. | | | |
| I choose when to separate a subordinate clause from a main clause with a comma. | | | |
| I use specialist vocabulary to suit my topic and reader. | | | |
| I learn the spellings and spelling patterns that I have trouble with so that I do not repeat the same mistakes. | | | |
| I check my drafts carefully so that I edit my work with the reader in mind. | | | |

 Now that you have reviewed your writing, record in your notebook the main things that you need to work on and improve. Keep checking your progress throughout the unit.

# Writing to inform, explain, describe: a newspaper article about the sinking of the Hood

This article, written by Simon Crerar, was published in *The Sunday Times* newspaper on December 16, 2001. Read the article (and the information contained in the diagrams on page 31) carefully a few times, and then you will have an opportunity to discuss it with your friends.

Do not worry if you do not understand every word immediately. A glossary of some words has been given at the end of the article. You may also need to use a dictionary to check the meaning of any other words you do not understand, or you could ask your teacher to explain these to you.

---

*The Sunday Times*   December 16, 2001

# The riddle of the Hood

1   It was the second year of the second world war, and the outlook was bleak. Britain, alone against the world, was struggling. On Empire Day, May 24, 1941, the embattled nation suffered a terrible blow. HMS Hood, the pride of the British fleet, was sunk in the north Atlantic by the German battleship Bismarck with enormous loss of life.

2   The implications were huge. For months London had been enduring nightly bombing during the blitz. Towns and cities across Britain were suffering, too. With the Bismarck poised to decimate the vital Atlantic shipping lanes, survival hung in the balance.

3   Why, though, did the mighty Hood sink so quickly? According to the two Admiralty inquiries of 1941, a shell from the Bismarck had penetrated the Hood's armour and detonated her aft magazines. But lingering doubts remained. Experts argued over the findings and some who testified claimed the Hood had sunk because a shell ignited her deck-stored torpedo warheads.

4   Now, 60 years after the sinking, an ambitious mission led by the American deep-sea explorer David Mearns and funded by Channel 4 has located the remains of the Hood. In the process it has found a new explanation for her sinking, and has laid a plaque to honour the 1,415 men lost.

5   The team draws a dramatic conclusion from its dive on the debris field almost two miles down: the Hood did not blow up once, as previously thought, but twice. The fatal shell from the Bismarck ignited the aft ammunition magazines, starting an inferno that spread below decks to set off the forward magazines, too.

6   "Two hundred tons of explosive going up is a huge explosion, almost like a small nuclear weapon," explains Dr Eric Grove, a naval historian who accompanied the search for the ship. "This accounts for there being only three survivors. The entire ship exploded."

7   Launched in August 1918, the battle cruiser HMS Hood was a 860ft, 48,360-ton reminder that Britannia ruled the waves. Yet from the beginning, she had a serious Achilles heel: despite extensive armour protecting her sides and forward deck, the lightly armoured aft deck made

the ship vulnerable to shells plunging from great height.

**8** In 1941, when Hitler realised that the blitz had failed to sap Britain's will, he planned to cut the country's supply lines by destroying the convoys from Canada and the United States. On May 19 his navy dispatched the Bismarck into the Atlantic. It was Hitler's newest and most mighty instrument of war, as equally well armed as the Hood but much more modern in design.

**9** On May 23 the Bismarck and her escort cruiser, the Prinz Eugen, were sighted in the Denmark Strait between Iceland and Greenland. Early the next day the Hood and her escort, the Prince of Wales, sighted the Bismarck at 17 miles and immediately engaged the Germans.

**10** Because of her vulnerability, Hood's captain, Vice-Admiral Lancelot Holland, had to move in close to avoid plunging shells. Hood opened fire first. Holland attempted to outpace the German ships so that he could turn the Hood broadside and bring her full complement of guns to bear.

**11** Shooting from a rolling, pitching platform was demanding—at sea only 1 in 100 shells generally hit their target. "Good gunnery counts in the long run," says Grove, "but in the fog of war, the outcome depends very much on how the gods are feeling that day."

**12** With only its fifth salvo the Bismarck hit the Hood's vulnerable aft deck. The shell detonated the ammunition magazines below and set off other explosions. Within minutes, she had sunk.

**13** Mearns's team sought permission from the Ministry of Defence to search for and film the Hood, and set sail on the survey vessel Northern Horizon. They located the wreck 9,200ft down and sent a Magellan 725 remotely operated vehicle to investigate the site. Video footage showed debris scattered over a wide area, with the bow of the Hood lying more than a mile and a half from the main hull.

**14** This discovery showed the "one explosion" theory of 1941 inquiries to be wrong. The dispersed debris provided evidence that two cataclysmic explosions seconds apart had ripped the Hood into three pieces.

**15** Grove claims that the Bismarck's shell ignited the 100 tons of cordite propellant in the aft magazines, which created "a massive deflagration that burnt its way like a blowlamp through the ship".

**16** When the fire reached the engine room vents, it shot upwards into the sky, says Grove, "but much also went forward through the machinery spaces, venting upwards around the bridge and igniting the forward magazines".

**17** Sailors on the Prince of Wales thought they saw signs of an explosion in a forward turret; according to German witnesses, a turret fired one last salvo as the Hood's bow rose into the air. In the light of Mearns's discoveries, it seems likely that these flames were exploding cordite rather than attempts to fire at the Bismarck.

**18** The loss of the Hood dealt a cruel blow to Britain's fragile confidence. Two hours after receiving news of the attack, Churchill responded by issuing his famous command: "Sink the Bismarck."

**19** On May 26, two days after the Hood was sunk, an aircraft spotted the Bismarck heading to France for repairs. Swordfish torpedo bombers launched from the Ark Royal hit the Bismarck three times, jamming her rudders. After bombardment from the Norfolk, King George V and Rodney, the paralysed Bismarck remained defiantly afloat. Eventually, boat-launched torpedoes and her crew's attempts to scuttle her sent Hitler's most fearsome ship to the bottom. Only 115 of her 2,246 men survived.

*Simon Crerar*

### Writing to inform, explain, describe

To support your reading of the article, here is a glossary of some of the words you may not have recognised.

**Glossary**
**decimate** (paragraph 2): destroy a large proportion of something
**ignited** (paragraph 3): set alight
**debris** (paragraph 5): scattered, broken pieces
**inferno** (paragraph 5): fire
**Achilles heel** (paragraph 7): weak point
**vulnerable** (paragraph 7): unprotected/exposed to danger
**detonated** (paragraph 12): exploded/caused to explode
**cataclysmic** (paragraph 14): violent or disastrous
**deflagration** (paragraph 15): sudden and rapid burning (a fire)
**bombardment** (paragraph 19): attack

## How do they do it?

Work in pairs or small groups to examine the following features of the article, and to discuss the questions asked.

- **The effective title:** *The riddle of the Hood* outlines the problem for the reader, particularly those who know of the Hood, and sets up the expectation that a solution may be offered. This engages the reader and creates interest in the article.

- **The diagrams:** For readers who may not have heard of the Hood, the pictures give clues about the content of the article. In the original article, in *The Sunday Times* newspaper, the pictures formed part of the overall impact of the article as they framed the text. There were two large pictures, which formed the top half of the article (see page 31). Two smaller pictures were inserted into the bottom centre part of the article. The pictures included:
  - statistical details about both the Bismarck and the Hood
  - a map showing where the encounter between the two ships occurred
  - diagrammatic explanations of the new theories.
  
  All of these work together with the text to support the reader in understanding the explanation offered.

- **The opening paragraph:** This sets the context for the reader, explaining the background to, and time of, the sinking of the ship. Identify the topic sentence in this paragraph. The opening is also emotive, with vocabulary choices such as *bleak, alone against the world, embattled nation, suffered a terrible blow* and *enormous loss of life*. What feelings do these quotations arouse in the reader? Why do you think the writer wished to create these particular feelings in the opening paragraph of his article?

- **The second paragraph:** The same atmosphere is continued in this next paragraph. Identify two or three quotations which help to develop this mood.

- **The third paragraph:** A question is now used, to raise the question many people asked at the time, and to draw the reader into the debate. The question makes the tone of the piece quite colloquial or friendly, as though the writer were talking directly to the reader. This paragraph outlines the answer provided in 1941, and then moves on to explain an alternative view. What connective is used to signal the introduction of the opposite viewpoint to the reader?

- **The new theory:** Paragraph 5 explains the new theory. Note the pair of commas, used to separate the comment, *as previously thought*. Here the pair of commas acts in the same way as a pair of brackets: the clause can be left out of the sentence and it will still make sense. Once you've read this paragraph, read the diagrammatic explanation again. What is the effect of giving the explanation twice (both in written form and as a diagram)?

- **Use of quotations:** Paragraph 6 gives the first of the quotations from Dr Eric Grove, a naval historian, who was part of the latest mission to find the remains of the Hood. What is the effect of including a quotation from an expert in his field?

**Writing to inform, explain, describe**

- **Use of a range of punctuation:** The article contains several examples of effective use of punctuation to aid meaning. Note the variety of punctuation used; to attain a Level 5⁺ you need to be able to use a range of punctuation accurately.

    - The article opens with **commas** being used for a variety of purposes. The first sentence has a **single comma** to separate two co-ordinating clauses: *It was the second year of the second world war, <u>and</u> the outlook was bleak*. The writer did not have to use a comma here; what is the effect of including the comma before the co-ordinator?

    - The final sentence of the second paragraph has a **single comma** used to separate the subordinate clause from the main clause: <u>With</u> *the Bismarck poised to decimate the vital Atlantic shipping lines, survival hung in the balance*. What is the effect of the comma in this sentence? Now find other examples of commas used to separate clauses in the article, and try to explain the reason for using the commas.

    - A third way in which **single commas** are used is to mark off a connective or phrase at the start of a sentence. There are several examples of these: *Now, … In 1941, … On May 23, … Because of her vulnerability, …* and *Eventually, …* Think about why the single comma has been used in each of these examples. How helpful are these commas?

    - The writer has also used **commas in pairs**, for example: *HMS Hood, the pride of the British fleet, was sunk in the north Atlantic by the German battleship Bismarck with enormous loss of life*. How does the pair of commas work in this sentence? (Think of what other punctuation could have been used instead of commas in this example.) Again, try to find other examples from the text where the writer has used a pair of commas for this reason.

    - Paragraphs 5 and 7 both contain a **colon**, which introduces ideas that expand on the point just made. Take a look at an example from the text: *The team draws a dramatic conclusion from its dive on the debris field almost two miles down: the Hood did not blow up once, as previously thought, but twice*. In this sentence the subject of the main clause which comes before the colon is a *dramatic conclusion*. Therefore, the clauses which follow the colon explain to the reader what this *dramatic conclusion* is. That is, the new finding that the Hood actually blew up twice. Now you do the same for the next colon, which is used in paragraph 7: identify the subject of the main clause which comes before the colon, and then explain how the use of the colon adds to the sentence. (Although this may seem difficult at first, keep working at it. Accurate use of a colon is one of the indicators of a writer who can achieve Level 5⁺.)

    - Paragraph 3 has a **question mark** (which has already been discussed earlier). Using a question is an effective way to draw your reader into your text; the reader feels as though they are being spoken to directly and therefore feels more involved in what's being discussed (see illustrated example of this over the page).

- Paragraphs 6, 11, 15 and 16 all contain **quotation marks**, to show quotations from Grove, punctuated in different ways. These paragraphs demonstrate a number of ways in which quotations can be effectively included in your writing. For each of these examples, identify how the dialogue has been used, and how it has been punctuated. Which of these is the most common form of including dialogue? Which is the most unusual? Which do you think is the most effective? Why? It is essential that you are able to include quotations in your writing, including your written responses to texts, and these need to be accurately punctuated for you to obtain Level 5+.

- **Apostrophes** to show possession have been used a number of times in the article, such as *Hood's armour, Mearn's team,* and *Britain's fragile confidence.* Give another reason when apostrophes should also be used. Now think of three examples of your own to show apostrophes used for possession.

- Paragraph 11 has a **dash** in the first sentence. Why do you think the dash has been used here? What is the effect of the dash? What other punctuation mark could have been used instead?

- Paragraph 17 has a **semi-colon** in the first sentence. A semi-colon is used to balance two equally weighted statements. It is stronger than a comma, but not as strong as a full stop. This is because the ideas in the two parts of the sentence are very closely linked together.

- **Variation of sentence length:** The writer mainly uses quite long sentences. He also varies his sentence length, though, and there are a number of examples of short sentences, used for effect, in the article: *The implications were huge.* (paragraph 2) *But lingering doubts remained.* (paragraph 3) *Within minutes, she had sunk.* (paragraph 12) *Only 115 of her 2,246 men survived.* (paragraph 19) Re-read the opening sentence of the second paragraph: *The implications were huge.* The author has used a short sentence here to allow the reader time to consider the wide-ranging consequences of the sinking of the Hood. The shorter sentence adds to the impact; it is more blunt and hard-hitting than the longer sentences.

For each of the other examples, think about why a short sentence was used, and the effect of the short sentence at this point. Next, take one of the long sentences from the article, and rewrite it as two or three short sentences. What is gained by doing this? What is lost? The important point is to sustain a balance between long and short sentences in your writing, and to use short sentences for particular effect.

- **Vocabulary choice and writing style:** Readers are more likely to take authors seriously if they respect them. When writing to inform, explain and describe, particularly if the writer is teaching the reader something, then it is important that the writer is believable. The author of this article achieves this in a variety of ways. Firstly, his use of evidence to support his explanation, such as the quotations from Dr Grove, shows us that he has researched his topic. Secondly, his vocabulary, with subject-specific and sophisticated words, helps to convince the reader that this person is educated and credible. The connectives and link phrases, such as *In the light of . . .* (paragraph 17), *According to . . .* (paragraph 3) and *In the process . . .* (paragraph 4), also help to make the writing sound measured and authoritative.

- **Passive verbs:** The author uses the passive quite often in his article. For example: *HMS Hood, the pride of the British fleet, was sunk in the north Atlantic by the German battleship Bismarck with enormous loss of life.* This is a useful construction, because instead of saying that the Bismarck sank the Hood, the author is saying that the Hood was sunk by the Bismarck. This is clever, because the Hood (the main subject of the article) remains the subject of the sentence.

- **Imagery:** Part of the success of writing to inform, explain and describe is the way in which the writer creates pictures in the reader's mind. This is helpful so that the reader is able to imagine, or visualise, what is being described. While we are used to authors using imagery in fiction texts, this is not always something we associate with non-fiction texts. However, including imagery can be equally suitable in a non-fiction text. Using imagery helps to draw the reader into the text; it helps us to personalise what we are reading and in this way makes it relevant to us. Imagery certainly adds to a reader's enjoyment of a text.

There are several examples of imagery used in the Hood article, three of which will be discussed here:

- The author quotes Grove who explains that the fire *burnt its way like a blowlamp through the ship* (paragraph 15). This simile is effective as it conveys the ferocity of the fire as it quickly and easily burnt through the ship. Now think of one or two different examples of similes of your own to describe an intense and powerful fire.

- The HMS Hood is personified in paragraph 7 when the writer describes the ship's vulnerable part as her *Achilles heel*. By using a metaphor associated with human weakness, the author is drawing parallels between the ship's weak points and ways in which we, too, can be attacked. Are there other ways in which weaknesses could be suggested through using metaphors or personification? Try to think of one or two examples of your own.

**Different examples of the Achilles heel**

- In the final paragraph, Simon Crerar writes: *the paralysed Bismarck remained defiantly afloat.* Using the adverb *defiantly* to describe how the ship remained afloat gives a specific character and attitude to the ship. This works, and the reader, therefore, admires the ship, just as the writer does. Now think of your own examples of negative conditions, such as illness or being in trouble, and then think of some adverbs to describe how people could respond to their state. As a final challenge in this section, try to write one or two metaphors of your own, where an inanimate object is personified in this way.

**The sports car relished its freedom by spinning round the bend**

## It's your turn

You are now going to research a topic and do your own writing to inform, explain and describe. Your task is to write a **newspaper article** about something mysterious or something which still has unanswered questions. The **aim** of your article is to provide information. This will consist of both background information and new information. You need to describe what the evidence is, give a logical explanation of what has happened, and explain any new theories or findings that have come to light. Your **audience** will be the newspaper's readers, who are mainly adults. As you have conducted research into your topic and want to be believed by your (adult) readers, you should aim for a fairly **formal** style.

While you are researching your topic, think about how you will present your ideas. For example, what **pictures** will you use? Would a **diagram** be helpful to illustrate a complex process? Think about what will make it easiest for your readers to follow your explanation.

Think, too, about what **evidence** you will use to support your views. Are you going to include **quotations** from experts? If so, you need to include these as part of your research.

### Choosing your topic

You could write about one of the following suggestions, or you could choose a topic of your own:
- the Loch Ness monster
- the Bermuda Triangle
- the Yeti
- the Marie Celeste
- the Beast of Bodmin
- the Roswell Incident.

### Conducting your research

To help you to plan your research, complete columns 1 to 3 of the grid below in as much detail as you can. Do not worry about column 4 for now.

| What do I **know** about my topic already? | What do I **want** to find out about the topic? What questions do I need to ask? | **Where** will I find the information? | What have I **learnt** from my research? What evidence will I be able to give the readers? |
|---|---|---|---|
|  |  |  |  |

Now you need to do your research, and then complete column 4 at the end of it.

# Planning and writing your article

- What **heading** will you use to attract your readers' attention? Do you need **sub-headings** as well? If so, what will these be?

- Think next about the **layout** and **presentation** of your article. What **pictures** or **diagrams** will you use? Where will these be positioned? What is their purpose? If they are helping to explain a process, what writing is needed in the diagrams? Are there any other presentational features you wish to include? If so, what purpose do they serve, and where will they be used?

- Next, you need to consider the **organisation** of your ideas. What order will your paragraphs be in? Is this the most effective way to organise them? Look at the structure that Simon Crerar followed in his article, as outlined in the table below.

| The Hood article | My article |
|---|---|
| Historical background | |
| Theories at the time | |
| The latest research | |
| New theories (from the research) | |
| Quotations from an expert | |
| More detail about the historical events | |

Now do the same and give a heading for each paragraph or group of paragraphs you will have in your article.

- Do you wish to include **imagery** in your article? Think about the impression you wish to give the reader of your subject. For example, do you want them to feel fearful, to have sympathy for the victims, or to feel angry about what happened? Would using imagery help your readers to respond in the way you want them to? Use the following table to think about some imagery you could include in your article – if it creates the right effect.

| Examples of a **simile** I could use ... |
|---|
| (A simile uses *like* or *as*: *the fire burnt like a blowlamp*.) |
| |

| Examples of a **metaphor** or **personification** I could use ... |
|---|
| (A metaphor is a direct comparison, which doesn't need *like* or *as*, and personification is a metaphor using human/living characteristics: *the train whistled in the tunnel; the paralysed Bismarck remained defiantly afloat*.) |
| |

- Where will you include **quotations** from experts to support your evidence? When including quotations, you may need to remind yourself of how to punctuate these properly.

- Once you have numbered your paragraphs, you now need to think about the **links** between them. What **connectives** will you use to show the reader the relationship between your ideas? Have you used a **range** of connectives? You will probably need to use some connectives to show time passing, such as *first, next, then, on May 23, later, in the afternoon;* and some to show cause and effect, such as *therefore, for this reason, as a result, consequently, because of.*

- Plan your **vocabulary** carefully. Remember that you wish to sound believable and authoritative. Here are some useful phrases, some of which include connectives, that you may wish to use when introducing ideas:

    *Evidence suggests ...*  
    *Contrary to popular opinion ...*  
    *A particularly crucial event ...*  
    *Additional research has proved ...*  
    *Recent data now indicates ...*  

    *A further aspect to consider ...*  
    *In the light of ...*  
    *Experts believe ...*  
    *Crucial evidence ...*  

- Think about **sentence length** carefully, and where you will use **short sentences for effect**. Most of your sentences will probably be quite long, as you will be using lots of subordination when you explain your ideas. However, it is a good idea to deliberately include a few short sentences for impact. Which points do you wish to particularly emphasise? Would a short sentence be useful here?

- Now consider **punctuation** carefully. By now you should be conscious of using **single commas** and **pairs of commas** more regularly in your sentences. (Remember that a **pair of commas** is placed around any extra information you are including in your sentence.) Is there any other punctuation you could use to add to the effect of your article? For example, is there somewhere where you could ask the reader a **question**, to draw them into your article? Do you need to use a **colon** at any stage, possibly to introduce a list?

- Before you start writing, think back to your **targets** for this chapter. Are there any other areas you need to focus on in particular detail?

Now you need to write your article, remembering to use your plan and to focus on applying your targets as you write.

## Revising your draft

When you've finished your draft, you need to work with a partner to revise it before you write a final version. Check over the following features:

- Is it **clear** what you have said? Ask your partner to read your draft. Ask them to mark places where they aren't sure what you mean. Ask them to mark places where the sentences don't follow on clearly.
- Have you used the right **verb tenses**?
- Have you written from a **viewpoint** that fits your text-type?
- Are your **pronouns** clear?

And:

- Have you ended each sentence with a **full stop**?
- Do all your sentences **begin with a capital letter**?
- Have you used **capital letters for names**?

And:

- Have you used an interesting **heading** for your article?
- Have you included **pictures** or **diagrams** to help your reader to understand complex ideas or explanations?
- Have you included **quotations** from experts to support your views? Are your quotations accurately punctuated?

And:

- Have you used a **single comma** to **mark off words and phrases** from the rest of the sentence? Have you also used single commas to separate items in a **list**?
- Have you used a **single comma** to separate **co-ordinate clauses**? Have you separated some of your **subordinate clauses** from main clauses with **commas**?
- Have you used a **pair of commas** to mark off words, phrases or even whole clauses, when they come in the middle of sentences?
- Have you used a **range of punctuation** to help your reader? For example, have you used a **colon, semi colon** or **question mark** in your article?
- Have you used a **range of connective words and phrases**?

And:

- Have you used a **topic sentence** when you start a new paragraph?
- Have you **developed** the topic sentence in the rest of the paragraph?
- Have you varied your **sentence length**? Have you included some **short sentences for effect**?
- Have you used interesting **vocabulary**?

And finally:

- Check your draft carefully for the **spelling patterns** you know you have trouble with.

## And you could try...

- Imagine that you witnessed a robbery on your way to school in the morning. Write a detailed, factual description of what you saw, giving as much relevant information as possible to help the police.
- Imagine you are the Headteacher of your school. You have to write a letter to the parents of the school informing them that the school's current arrangement of term and holiday dates is going to change. Explain what the changes will be, and give the reasons for these changes.
- Design a poster for the movie that is being produced about your favourite book. Then, write an explanation of your poster, explaining why you selected that particular image.
- You have decided that you need more pocket money but your parents don't agree with you. You have tried persuading them, but you know they respond best when presented with information to consider. Write down ten key ideas which you will use to inform them of the reasons why you need more money. Remember to present them with your information in an adult way.
- You have organised a weekend away on a camping trip. You are going to meet the people who will be going with you. Prepare notes to take with you to the meeting. You need to describe where they will be going and what the facilities are; give them information about what they will need to take with them; and explain any safety procedures they will need to follow.
- Your group has been given an assignment to research the positive and negative effects of cloning. People in your group don't know what cloning is. You have a computer at home, so have volunteered to find out and then explain the process to them the following day. Write the explanation you will give them.

# Unit Three

## Writing to persuade, argue, advise

**In this unit, you will:**

- think about what is special about writing to persuade, argue, advise

- review your own writing, to see what needs to be done to make it a sound Level 5+

- look at how professional authors write newspaper opinion columns and editorials to persuade, argue, advise

- draft your own writing in these forms.

Main National Framework Objectives Covered: 7Sn1, 7Sn8, 7Sn13d/e/f, 7Sn15, 7Wr1, 7Wr15, 8Sn1, 8Sn6, 8Sn10, 8Wr2, 8Wr14, 9Wr14

# Writing to persuade, argue, advise – what is it?

This kind of writing is very common both in and outside school. If we look at each aspect separately, we can see that:

- Writing to **persuade** should make readers see things from the writer's point of view. It uses emotive language to work on the reader's feelings. It repeats words (repetition) and asks rhetorical questions to make the writer's point strongly. It gives detailed examples to help readers understand what the writer means.
- Writing to **argue** should persuade a reader with a logical argument. It persuades by giving reasons and detailed explanations. It also persuades by discussing opposite viewpoints. It then shows where they are wrong.
- Writing to **advise** should make the reader want to follow the instructions given. It often persuades the reader by sounding friendly and informal. However, if the writing sounds formal, it can persuade because it seems important, speaking with authority.

In this unit, you will study two pieces of writing, taken from newspapers, each of which will cover all three aspects of writing to persuade, argue and advise. To help you think further about the features of this kind of writing, discuss the following text-types. Which ones are meant to persuade? Which ones are meant to argue or to advise? Sometimes, they may do more than one of these things, like the texts you will study in this unit. Discuss the list and see what you think.

a science fiction novel
a newspaper report on a volcanic explosion
a novel set in the Middle Ages
a recipe for lasagne
a private diary
a newspaper editorial
an instruction manual for a video
an advertisement for a supermarket
an essay about 'Macbeth'
a cricketer's autobiography

a leaflet from Friends of the Earth
a war story
a letter to your local council, complaining about the lack of safe routes for cyclists
a report on an experiment in science
a letter from a friend who has moved away
an essay in History about the causes of World War One
a letter to a newspaper about vandalism
your favourite joke

# What makes a good piece of writing to persuade, argue, advise?

You now have a general idea about what the range of writing to persuade, argue and advise is like. For homework, collect as many examples of these types of writing as you can. Look in newspapers and magazines. Look at recipes and instruction manuals. Collect leaflets from shops, local council offices, or tourist offices. Look through the writing you do at school. Look at writing in other subjects, as well as in English.

Working in groups, look at the examples you have collected. Remember what you know about non-fiction text-types. What **features** of writing to persuade, argue and advise can you pick out? Do you think that some of your examples get their ideas across more clearly or more strongly than others? Can you explain why?

Look for:

- how the writer catches the reader's attention at the start
- the viewpoint chosen by the writer. Is it first person (*I/we*) or third person (*he/she/it/they*)?
- how the writer addresses (speaks to) the reader
- how informal (more like speech) or formal (more like writing) the voice of the writer sounds
- the persuasive techniques used by the writer. Look for emotive language, repetition, or rhetorical questions
- the main tense used by the writer
- any use of modal verbs (*must, should, can,* and so on)
- different sentence lengths
- the range of connectives which the writer uses
- when the writer starts new paragraphs
- how the writer develops the topic sentence of paragraphs. Look for extra detail or examples.

As a class, make up a list of the features that you would expect to find in writing to persuade, argue and advise. Don't worry at this stage about how the features affect meaning. Just collect a list of features. You will see how these features are used, later in the unit.

Record the list in your notebook. You might present what you have learnt as a wall display.

# How can you improve your own writing?

Collect two or three pieces of your own writing to persuade, argue and advise. Talk to your partner. How many of the features do you use already? What features do you need to improve?

On this and the following page, there are grids which show in detail the things you need to do for a sound Level 5+. There are a lot of things to think about, but don't worry. A lot of them you will already be doing well. Some, though, you will need to improve on. The grids will help you think about what to improve. If you are not sure about a feature, your teacher will be able to explain. You could also wait to see how the feature is used later in the unit.

Copy the grids into your notebook. (It may also be possible for your teacher to photocopy them.) For each feature, put a tick in the box which applies to you. When you have finished, you will be able to see what you need to focus on in the rest of this unit. You will then be able to track your targets and improvements as you write.

| FEATURES OF WRITING | I can do this sometimes | I can usually do this | I need to improve this |
|---|---|---|---|
| I capture the reader's interest with a heading or opening sentence. | | | |
| I know how to choose a personal (*I/we*) or impersonal (*he/she/it/they*) viewpoint. | | | |
| I make sure that it's clear what pronouns refer back to. | | | |
| I know when to speak to the reader in a formal or informal way. | | | |
| I have a clear idea of who the reader is, and how I want them to react. | | | |
| I choose formal or informal words where I need to. | | | |
| I use emotive language to persuade the reader. | | | |
| I use repetition to persuade the reader. | | | |
| I use rhetorical questions to persuade the reader. | | | |
| I know when verbs are in the past or present tense. | | | |
| I don't vary verb tenses unless there is a good reason. | | | |

# Writing to persuade, argue, advise

| FEATURES OF WRITING | I can do this sometimes | I can usually do this | I need to improve this |
|---|---|---|---|
| I use modal verbs. | | | |
| I end sentences with a full stop and start them with a capital letter. | | | |
| I write names with a capital letter. | | | |
| I write short sentences for emphasis. | | | |
| I separate words, phrases and clauses in sentences with a single comma. | | | |
| I separate words, phrases and clauses in sentences with a pair of commas. | | | |
| I choose when to separate a subordinate clause from a main clause with a comma. | | | |
| I use a range of connectives to begin subordinate clauses. | | | |
| I use a range of connectives to link sentences and paragraphs. | | | |
| I use logical connectives to structure an argument. | | | |
| I start a new paragraph to show a change in topic. | | | |
| I start a new paragraph to show a change in time. | | | |
| I use a topic sentence for each paragraph. | | | |
| I develop the topic sentence by explaining in detail or by giving examples. | | | |
| I keep a list of the spellings and spelling patterns that I have trouble with. | | | |
| I check my drafts carefully for the spellings and patterns I have trouble with. | | | |

Now that you have reviewed your writing, record in your notebook the main things that you need to work on and improve. Keep checking your progress throughout the unit.

## Writing to persuade, argue, advise: newspaper opinion columns

Opinion columns are like newspaper letters in many ways. The writers put forward their personal opinions about an issue. They want to **persuade** the reader to agree with them. However, the writers of opinion columns also **argue** for their point of view by looking at what other people think about the topic. This makes their opinion look stronger, because they have tested it against other viewpoints. At the end of their argument, also, they will usually give **advice** about what should be done to make things better.

Read the following opinion article, which is adapted from one by Quentin Willson, writing in *The Mirror*, August 14, 2001.

---

*The Mirror* August 14, 2001

### Bad driving is the real killer

Speed does kill. Only a fool would argue otherwise. But the astonishing clamour over using cameras to enforce speed limits has reached crisis levels. The Government has handled the debate badly. As a result, there's a danger that speed cameras could drive a wedge between the public and the police.

The Government has failed to convince 25 million motorists that speed cameras do actually save a significant number of lives. Last year, road fatalities fell by just 14. Fourteen lives are always worth saving, but to claim it is due solely to speed cameras is to tell a whopper of some magnitude. Has the Government considered improved car safety? What about airbags, side impact beams, or ABS brakes? Could the fact that modern cars are the safest they've ever been have some bearing on road fatalities?

It is a fact that, because of improved safety, fewer people are seriously injured or dying in cars, yet neither the Government nor the police mention this important fact. They also fail to mention that, since speed cameras were introduced, the average annual number of road fatalities has actually gone up.

Last week, I had a conversation with an assistant chief constable, who admitted he has no fixed speed cameras in his county because he doesn't believe they work. He is horrified that so much time and energy are being wasted on the subject, and believes police efforts would be better directed towards the real killer on our roads – bad driving, which, bizarrely, never gets a mention. If we created a clear and intelligent strategy to improve the nation's driving skills, the number of road fatalities would fall overnight.

*Quentin Willson*

---

## How do they do it?

- **Catching the reader's attention.** Quentin Willson starts with two short statement sentences. Saying *Speed does kill* rather than *Speed kills* makes the first statement stronger. What effect does the second statement sentence (*Only a fool . . .*) have? The impression it gives you of the writer is that he is not a fool. How would that impression help persuade the reader?

- **Making it personal.** Because it's an opinion piece, Quentin Willson uses the first-person pronoun (*I*), and refers to his own experiences. Referring to his experiences makes his writing persuasive, because he is giving reasons to back up his opinions. He also asks the reader questions. What would be the effect of these questions on the reader?

- **Formal or informal?** Abbreviations (such as *they've* instead of *they have*) make writing sound more informal, and more like speech. How many can you find in this article? Pronouns are also important in making language sound formal or informal. Count how often Quentin Willson uses the first-person viewpoint (*I*), compared with the more formal third-person viewpoint (*he/she/it/they*)? He also uses slang words like *whopper*, which sounds informal. However, he chooses formal words and phrases like *fatalities*, *of some magnitude*, or *had a conversation with*. What words and phrases would he have used instead, if he had wanted to be informal? Overall, the mixture of formal and informal writing is persuasive, because the writer seems friendly (informal style), but speaks with authority (formal style).

- **The structure of the article.** Now look at the way the article is put together:
  - The first paragraph **sets out** the problem that the writer is arguing about. He is arguing against the attitude of the government to using speed cameras. The short sentences give a dramatic start. He uses emotive language such as *Only a fool*, *astonishing clamour* and *drive a wedge* to persuade his readers. Pick out other emotive words and phrases. Replace these emotive words and phrases with plainer, less emotive ones. What effect does the plainer version have on us, compared to the original?
  - The second and third paragraphs **develop** the point set out in the first one. There, Quentin Willson argued against the attitude of the Government to speed cameras. Here, he gives reasons for his viewpoint. Look at the way he persuades his reader by quoting facts and statistics. Why is that effective? He also gives lists of detailed examples to back up his point. List each example in your notebook. Discuss why each one is persuasive.
  - The last paragraph **concludes** the argument. The writer gives another example to back up his view. Why would this example be so persuasive? He then **advises** by putting forward a recommendation about what should be done. Why does he use the pronoun *we* in this last sentence?
  - Notice the **connectives**. When you argue a point of view, trying to persuade your reader, the connectives help you signpost your argument clearly. *But* tells you that the writer is going to put an opposing point of view to what he has just said. *If,*

*yet*, *also*, and *because* are other useful connectives for an argument. What job do they do in this article? Look also at *As a result*. What kind of information does this phrase give you? What other connectives can you think of, that would help you in a logical argument?

- Quentin Willson often uses a **single comma** to separate **co-ordinate clauses** (beginning with *and/but/or*) from the **main clause** of a sentence.

**Fourteen lives are always worth saving, <u>but</u> to claim it is due solely to speed cameras is to tell a whopper of some magnitude.**

He could also have chosen to start a sentence with *but*:

**Only a fool would argue otherwise. <u>But</u> the astonishing clamour over using cameras to enforce speed limits has reached crisis levels.**

What is the effect of choosing to start a sentence with this word?

- He also often chooses to use a **single comma** to separate **subordinate clauses** from the main clause of a sentence. (Subordinate clauses begin with all the other connectives apart from *and/but/or*. For example, you may have already come across subordinating connectives like *because/although/if/when/where/after/before*. Subordinate clauses can also begin with words such as *which/who/that*.) Here is a subordinate clause separated from the main clause by a single comma:

**<u>If</u> we created a clear and intelligent strategy to improve the nation's driving skills, the number of road fatalities would fall overnight.**

- However, Quentin Willson sometimes chooses not to separate the subordinate clause from the main clause. In the following example, he chooses to mark off one subordinate clause with a comma, but not the other.

**Last week, I had a conversation with an assistant chief constable, <u>who</u> admitted he has no fixed speed cameras in his county <u>because</u> he doesn't believe they work.**

- Why does Quentin Willson put a comma in front of *who*, but not in front of *because*? Find other examples of subordinate clauses which he marks with commas. Then find examples where he doesn't use a comma. Can you see any reasons for the differences?
- There are two other uses of **single commas** to notice. The first is to mark off words or phrases from the rest of the sentence, as in the example above (*Last week, I had a conversation ...*). How many other examples can you find? Can you explain what is the effect of using a comma in this way? The writer also uses a single comma to separate the individual items in a list. There is one list in this article. Can you find it?
- Another way in which Quentin Willson uses **commas** is to use them **in pairs**, around words, phrases, or even whole clauses. For example:

*They also fail to mention that, since speed cameras were introduced, the average annual number of road fatalities has actually gone up.*

- Can you find two other examples of places where Quentin Willson uses a pair of commas? What is the effect of doing that? What kind of information do the words between the commas give?
- Finally, notice the **modal verbs** *would* and *could*. Words like this are useful in persuasive arguments. Here, they suggest possibilities – things that might happen, under certain conditions. Notice the use of the verb *do,* to emphasise the point of the topic sentence in the second paragraph. Notice, too, the **verb tenses**. The writer uses the present tense for general statements or statements of truth. How many of these can you find? He also uses the past tense when talking about things that have happened in the past. He then uses these past events to give evidence or proof for what he is saying.

## It's your turn

Now draft a newspaper opinion article of your own. It could be an article from a newspaper like *The Mirror*, or it could fit into a paper for young people, like *The Newspaper*. It should be four paragraphs and about 300–400 words in length. It should put forward a persuasive argument about something which you think is wrong and should be changed. It should also use the range of techniques which you have studied in Quentin Willson's article on page 48.

**Think back** to your targets before you begin. What are your personal targets for improvement? Remember, in particular, to be aware of how you are using commas throughout your article.

- The first thing you will need to do is find a topic for your article. You may already have a subject that you feel strongly about, and want to improve or change. You may even have clear ideas about what you think should be done about it. If not, you will see suggestions on page 60 which may help you to find ideas.
- When you have chosen a topic on which to write, try to collect as many examples, reasons and viewpoints as you can. You will probably be writing about a topic from your own experiences, so you could include things that have happened to you. You could also include facts about what people do, or say. Referring to the views of people you know (parents? friends? teachers?) would be persuasive, too.
- Make sure that you have got notes on the opposite viewpoint to your own. Quentin Willson argues against the Government's viewpoint. What are the views that you will argue against? You might like to use a table like the one below to help you set out views for and against your opinion.

| I think that: | Some people (can you say who?) think that: |
|---|---|
| • | • |
| • | • |
| Examples/reasons/views/facts to support my opinion: | Examples/reasons/views/facts from the opposite side: |
| • | • |
| • | • |
| • | • |
| • | |

- Now draft your **opening paragraph**:
  - In this paragraph, summarise what you are going to say overall. This overview will be helpful for the reader. It helps them follow what you are going to say. Don't go into detail, though. Only write between three and five sentences at the most.
  - Capture the reader's attention with the topic sentence. Make the opening sentence short and punchy. You could open with a question. What effect would that have? Could you use any emotive words and phrases to help persuade your reader?
  - Remember to use a first-person viewpoint (*I*), because you are giving your own opinion. You will also be referring to your own experiences. Aim for a style which is a mixture of formal (more like writing) and informal (more like speech). How does Quentin Willson mix formal and informal styles?
  - When you have written your opening paragraph, just check to see if you could put any single commas between clauses. Or start a sentence with a co-ordinator. Effect?

- Develop your ideas in the **second paragraph**:
  - In this paragraph, put forward your main argument. You could begin your topic sentence with *I feel that...* or *I think that...*
  - After your topic sentence, write four or five sentences which back up your opinion with facts, viewpoints or examples, or which explain your reasons in more detail. Useful connectives to signpost the reader through the paragraph: *first, second, to begin with, next, also, if, therefore, for example.*
  - What modal verbs would be useful at this point? Some examples: *could, would, should, might, may, must, ought.* Remind yourself of what each one means.
  - What persuasive techniques could you make use of in this paragraph? What about questions to the reader? Lists of detailed examples? Facts and statistics? Emotive language?
  - Look also at your commas. Where do you have a choice to put in single commas? Will you choose to do so, or not? Are there any words or phrases which you need to mark off with a single comma? If you have used a list, have you separated the individual items with single commas? Could you try using a pair of commas in one of your sentences? What sort of information goes between a pair of commas? Effect?

- In the **third paragraph**, you will develop your ideas further by looking at the opposite point of view. You will put forward views against what you have already said. Then you will explain why these views are wrong.
    - You could start your topic sentence with *Some people think that* ... or *An opposite view is that* ... Then give facts, examples, or further details in the next couple of sentences.
    - About halfway through the paragraph, say why you think these views are wrong. You could say *However, I think* ...
    - Useful connectives, (apart from *however*) are: *on the other hand, in spite of this, in contrast, instead, otherwise, therefore, as a result*. These connectives will help signpost your reader through the paragraph.
    - Try a couple of modal verbs. Some examples: *could, would, should, might, may, must, ought*. Which ones from this list would fit in?
    - Think about where you could put in single commas. If possible, you could also try using a pair of commas within one of your sentences. Be aware of the effect of putting in commas – either single ones, or in a pair.

- In the **final paragraph**, you will sum up your argument, and give advice about what you think should happen.
    - You could start your topic sentence with a connective such as *overall, to sum up, in conclusion*. Other useful connectives: *also, too, however, therefore, as a result*.
    - You could bring in your most convincing example or piece of evidence, at this point. What would it be?
    - This paragraph is an ideal place to use modal verbs, such as *must, ought, should*. These verbs show that you are saying what you think should happen. Compare them with the other modals which are listed earlier. Which modals are as strong as *must/ought/should*? Which ones are weaker?
    - This paragraph is also the final chance to look over your single commas. Are there any places where you can choose to separate subordinate or co-ordinate clauses from the main clause with a single comma? Effect? Are there words or phrases to mark off from the rest of the clause with a single comma? Any lists? What about using a pair of commas?

- And what about a **title** for your article? The best time to think of one, probably, is when you've finished your first draft, and you're fairly clear about what you want to say. Remember that the title helps attract the reader, hooking them into reading the rest of the article. It sums up your viewpoint in a short, punchy sort of way. Would a humorous tone fit your approach?

## Writing to persuade, argue, advise: newspaper editorials

This type of persuasive writing uses many of the techniques used in opinion columns. In an editorial (or leading article) newspaper editors put forward their opinions about important issues. They try to **persuade** their readers with logical **argument**. They may also give **advice** on how things could be improved. However, editorials are more formal in their language than opinion columns. They speak with authority, in an impersonal way, because they give the views of the newspaper, not just the opinions of one person. Here is an example from the *Daily Express*, about the National Health Service helpline which people can use to discuss their health over the phone.

*Daily Express*, August 6, 2001

# Helpline needs doctoring

NHS Direct was a good idea. The 24-hour health helpline means that the public has access to expert medical information, day and night, without needing to add to the queues at surgeries and hospitals. It should reassure people with trivial complaints that they do not need medical attention, while encouraging those who need it to see a doctor, when they might not otherwise have bothered.

Unfortunately, it isn't working out quite as planned. GPs and hospital doctors say NHS Direct is actually increasing their workloads by encouraging patients to seek treatment unnecessarily. One doctor claims to have been called out to see patients suffering from colds or slightly raised temperatures.

The problem seems to be that the system's computer is not always flexible enough to distinguish between serious conditions, and trivial conditions with some similar symptoms. It must surely be possible to rectify this, and improve the accuracy of the diagnoses. Equally, GPs must have the resources to deal with all the genuine cases referred to them.

## How do they do it?

- **Catching the reader's attention.** The headline sums up what the editorial will say. It's short, with what kind of word missing? Why do they miss it out? There's a pun – a play on words – in the headline, too. Can you explain it?

- **Formal or informal?** Informal writing often sounds close to speech. An editorial, on the other hand, needs to sound formal. This gives it authority, and makes it persuasive. It sounds formal by:

- avoiding abbreviations. (How many can you find?)
- using formal words, such as *rectify* instead of *put right*, or *has access to* instead of *can get*
- using a lot of words with three syllables or more. (How many can you find? Could you replace them with simpler, shorter words? Try using a thesaurus and dictionary to help you with this.)
- using a third-person viewpoint (*he/she/it/they*), which makes it sound impersonal. Try rewriting in an informal way a couple of the sentences from this article, using the ideas above. Does your new version sound as if it has less authority?

● **Structuring the article.** Look at how the article is put together:
- The <u>first paragraph</u> **sets out** the good points about NHS Direct. The topic sentence is a short, simple statement, which catches the reader's attention. What does the use of the past tense tell you, though? The editor then **develops** the topic sentence, explaining, in the next two sentences, what he means in more detail. Notice the present tense, which is used to make statements about things that are true at the present time. Notice also the modal verb *should*. What does that tell you about how the argument will continue in the later paragraphs?
- The <u>second paragraph</u> puts an **alternative view**. The topic sentence begins with the connective *unfortunately*. This tells us that a contrast is coming later in the paragraph. The next two sentences develop the point made in the topic sentence. They point out the weaknesses that they see in NHS Direct. They give **examples** of what the writer means. Again, the writer uses the present tense to make general statements about things that appear to be true.
- The topic sentence of the <u>final paragraph</u> **analyses** the problem *(seems to be that ...)*. The next two sentences bring the editorial to a **conclusion**. They **advise** or **recommend** what should be done. Notice the modal verb *must*, which is used twice. Why is it used here? Notice also the connectives *surely* and *equally*. What effect would they have on the reader?

● Remind yourself of how Quentin Willson uses **commas**. In this editorial, there is only one example of **commas in a pair**. Can you find that example? What is the effect of using a pair of commas like this? Now look at the different ways of using **single commas** in this editorial.

## It's your turn

Draft a newspaper leading article, using the techniques you have just studied. If you need help with finding topics to write about, there are suggestions on page 60. When you have chosen a topic, start to collect examples to back up and develop your points. In each paragraph, try to find at least two examples to illustrate the point you are making in the topic sentence.

When you draft your article, write three paragraphs, each of about 70–80 words. **Think back** to your targets, and **review** what you have learnt.

- Set out your main point in the **first paragraph.**
  - Keep your language formal. This will be persuasive because it sounds authoritative. Use a third-person viewpoint. Avoid abbreviations. Choose more formal, three-syllable words rather than shorter, simpler words. (Use a dictionary and thesaurus to help you.)
  - Make the topic sentence a simple statement. Then use the sentences which follow to explain in more detail, and to give examples.
  - Keep mainly to the present tense, because you are making statements about things which are true at the present time. You could try one or two modal verbs, like *should* or *might*.
  - Use connectives to signpost the reader through your paragraph, – *first, also, for instance, for example*.
  - Remember to check commas.

- Use the **second paragraph** to put the alternative view.
  - Your topic sentence should make a contrast with what you have said before. Connectives like *however, on the other hand* or *alternatively* might be useful.
  - Give examples in the following sentences to develop the point. Use connectives like *for instance, for example*. If you are explaining what might happen, try connectives like *therefore, as a result*, or *in that case*.
  - Check verb tenses, formal language, and commas.

- The **final paragraph** makes your recommendations about what should be done.
  - You might start the paragraph by analysing the problem in greater detail, or by commenting on the alternative view. Connectives like *to sum up, all in all, overall, in conclusion* would be useful. You might also use *consequently*, or *as a result* to explain what might happen.
  - Because you are giving advice at this stage, you will need to use modal verbs such as *should, ought, must*.
  - Remember to check verb tenses, formal language, and commas.

- Finally, think of a **title** which will attract the reader's attention, and which summarises what you're going to say. Keep words to a minimum. What kinds of words usually get left out in headlines?

# Revising your drafts

When you've finished your drafts, you need to work with a partner to revise them before you write a final version. Check over the following features:

- Is it **clear** what you have said? Ask your partner to read your drafts. Ask them to mark places where they aren't sure what you mean. Ask them to mark places where the sentences don't follow on clearly.
- Have you used the right **verb tenses**? (Mainly present tense. If you use past or future time, make sure you know why.)
- Have you written from a **viewpoint** that fits your text-type? (First person for opinions, or third person for editorials.)
- Have you used a range of **persuasive techniques**? (For example, emotive language, detailed examples, questions to the reader, sounding authoritative.)
- Are your **pronouns** clear? (Ask your partner to read your drafts, highlighting each pronoun. If they aren't sure what the pronoun refers back to, they should put a question mark in the margin. You'll then need to make it clear.)

And:

- Have you ended each sentence with a **full stop**? (Count the number of sentences you have written in each paragraph. Write the number in the margin. Then count the number of full stops. The numbers should be the same!)
- Do all your sentences **begin with a capital letter**? (Underline the first word of each sentence. Has it got a capital letter?)
- Have you used **capital letters for names**? (Underline each name in what you have written. Put a ring round the first letter. Is it a capital?)

And:

- Have you used a **single comma** to **mark off words and phrases** from the rest of the sentence? (For example, *Equally, GPs must have ...*) A single comma is also used to separate items in a **list**. (For example, *What about air bags, side impact bars, or ABS brakes?*)
- Have you used a **single comma** to separate **co-ordinate clauses**? (Look for places where you've used the **co-ordinators** *and/but/or* to begin clauses. Put a box round the co-ordinator at the start of the clause. Have you put a comma in front of the co-ordinator?)
- Have you separated some of your **subordinate clauses** from main clauses with **single commas**? (Look at the start of each clause to see if it begins with a **subordinator** – for example, *because, since, as, so, so that, to, in order to, how, if, unless, although, instead of, who, why, which, that, how*. If there is a subordinator, put a box around it. Do you need to use a comma to separate the subordinate clause from the main clause? What would be the effect of doing that?)
- Have you used a **pair of commas** to mark off words, phrases or even whole clauses, when they come in the middle of sentences? For example:

*They also fail to mention that, since speed cameras were introduced, the average annual number of road fatalities has actually gone up.*

- Have you used a **range of connective words and phrases**? (Look at the connectives you have marked. Don't overuse **co-ordinators** such as *and* or *but*. Make sure you have used a range of **subordinators**. Check also that you have used a range of connective words and phrases which help to **signpost** your argument clearly. Here are some words and phrases which will help you to list your points: *first, second, to begin with, furthermore, next;* or to summarise: *all in all, to conclude, to sum up, overall, altogether;* or to give examples: *in other words, for instance, for example;* or to write about results: *therefore, consequently, as a result;* or to explain what might happen: *otherwise, in that case;* or to contrast: *rather, on the other hand, alternatively, instead, however.*)

And:
- Have you used a **topic sentence** when you start a new paragraph? (Underline the topic sentence in each paragraph.)
- Have you **developed** the topic sentence in the rest of the paragraph? (Mark with the words *Explain* or *Example* the sentences which follow the topic sentence. This will help you see how each sentence develops the topic of the paragraph.)

And finally:
- Check your drafts carefully for the **spelling patterns** you know you have trouble with. (Use your spelling list to remind you.)

When you are ready, review your progress using the grids from pages 46 and 47. What features of writing have you improved? The more improvements you have made, the closer you are to a sound Level 5⁺.

## And you could try ...

- Finding topics to write about is not always easy. However, you could do a number of things to discover and develop ideas:
    - You could talk to your friends, and to other people in your class. Is there anything which they are interested in, or which they have a strong opinion about? It's probably best to stick to topics connected with your life at school, or in your community. If you concentrate on your own experiences, and the experiences of young people of your own age, you will have examples that you can use to illustrate your arguments. You will also be speaking as an expert, which will make your advice convincing.
    - You could use a range of writing techniques to help you find ideas to write about. For example, you could write a 'brainstorm' list of ideas that come to mind. It doesn't matter how strange they sound – just write continuously for a minute or two, going for as many words or ideas as you can. Don't stop writing; it's important to keep your pen moving, to keep the ideas flowing. You can then pick the best ideas afterwards.
    - You could also find ideas by writing for 6 or 7 minutes without stopping. Again, keep the ideas flowing by keeping your pen moving. You could start with something like *What I would like to improve/change/stop is* ... Try to include explanations, reasons and examples in what you write. When you finish, look back over what you have written. Underline the ideas which you think would be useful.

- Another idea to help you find topics for writing opinion columns or editorials might be to look for issues covered in national newspapers. You might also find them from watching TV or listening to the radio. Think, too, about issues in your own school or local area.

- Look at the editorial and letter pages of a few newspapers. Very often, you will have a double-page spread of editorials, letters, and at least one opinion article. You could work with a group to produce a double-page spread like this. Base it on one newspaper, and keep to that newspaper's style of presentation. If you have access to a desktop publishing package, you could try to get the page and layout looking like the original.

- You could use the newspapers you have collected to research commas. Remind yourself of the various ways in which single and paired commas are used. Pick two or three pages, and count the number of paired commas used. What is the effect of marking off these words, phrases or clauses with a pair of commas? Now look at the single commas. How many can you find, which mark off words or phrases from the rest of the sentence? How many commas can you find, which separate items in a list? Finally, count the number of co-ordinate and subordinate clauses which are separated from the main clause by a single comma. Then count the number which do not use a comma. Look at four or five examples, and explain what effect the writer's choice has had on the meaning.

- Finally, here's an introduction to the use of **passive verbs**. You will need to know more about them in the next book. The notes below, and the examples from Quentin Willson's article, will help you to spot passives, and to think about the effect they have on meaning.

| Subject | Auxiliary Verb | Past Participle |
| --- | --- | --- |
| *fewer people* | *are* | *injured* |
| *more speed cameras* | *were* | *introduced* |
| *time and energy* | *are being* | *wasted* |
| *police efforts* | *would be* | *directed* |

Can you work out the rules for forming passives? You tend to find passives in formal writing. They give an impersonal feeling to the text. Find the above examples in the article, and work out why they give this impersonal feeling. (A clue: can you tell who or what is doing the action of the verb to the subject – for example, injuring the people, or introducing the cameras?) Can you find an example of a passive verb in the *Daily Express* editorial?

# Unit Four

## *Writing to analyse, review, comment*

**In this unit, you will:**

- think about what is special about writing to analyse, review, comment

- review your own writing, to see what needs to be done to make it a sound Level 5+

- look at how professional authors write to analyse, review and comment on a book, a film, an important issue or subject of general interest

- draft your own writing in these forms.

Main National Framework Objectives Covered: 7Sn1a/b/c, 7Sn3, 7Wr18, 7Wr19, 8Sn1, 8Sn2, 8Wr16, 8Wr17, 8Wr18

## Writing to analyse, review, comment – what is it?

When you write to **analyse**, **review** and **comment**, you might be writing about a very wide range of things. The thing you are writing about is called the **subject matter**. The subject matter might be:

- a new book, poem or book of poetry; a new film or video, song or television programme
- a sports event, like the England football team's progress in the World Cup; an historical event, like the Battle of Hastings; a scientific discovery, like a new drug to fight against cancer; or a human achievement, like the first ascent of a difficult mountain
- an issue, like whether school uniform is a good thing; or a speech by a politician, on a subject of great national importance, like whether Britain should join the euro.

Whatever the subject matter is, this kind of writing has three main features.

- The writing **reviews** its subject matter. This means the writing describes or explains the subject so that the reader understands it. If it is a new book, the writing will explain briefly what the story is, if it is an historical event, the writing will explain what happened. If is an issue it will explain what the issue is about.
- The writing will **analyse** the subject matter. This means picking out what is good or bad about it. If it is a book, the writing will say what was interesting and different about the book. It will say what was boring or predictable about it. If it is an event, it will say why something was important or significant about it. If it is an issue where people have very different views, it will say what are the advantages and disadvantages of each viewpoint.
- The writing will **comment** on the subject matter. This means that it will give the writer's own opinions about the book, event, or issue, backed up with evidence.

When writing to **analyse**, **review** and **comment**, the writer always has to remember what the reader wants to know. Its **purpose** is not just to give the writer's own opinions, but also to help the reader make up his or her mind about whether to watch a new film, buy a new book, or vote to join the euro. Writing to **analyse**, **review** and **comment** might be written in a formal or informal style. The writer needs to decide whether a formal style will help make the subject seem serious or whether an informal, chatty style will make his subject more appealing to a certain type of audience.

# Writing to analyse, review, comment

 Discuss the following text-types. Which ones are meant to analyse, review and comment? Discuss the list and see what you think.

a science fiction novel
a private diary
a scientific report on a new drug to fight flu
a newspaper comment on the Government's plans for the Railways
a novel set in the Middle Ages
an instruction manual for a video
a recipe for lasagne
a magazine article about three new cookery books
an advertisement for a supermarket
a report on two supermarkets' own brand chocolate bars
an essay about the Harry Potter books
a cricketer's autobiography
a leaflet from Friends of the Earth on the effects of building new nuclear power stations
a letter from a friend who has moved away
an essay in History about the Battle of Hastings
a speech by a politician on how schools can be made better
a letter to a newspaper about vandalism
a letter to your local council, complaining about the lack of safe routes for cyclists
your favourite joke
a report on an experiment in science
a page in a teenage magazine about new films and videos

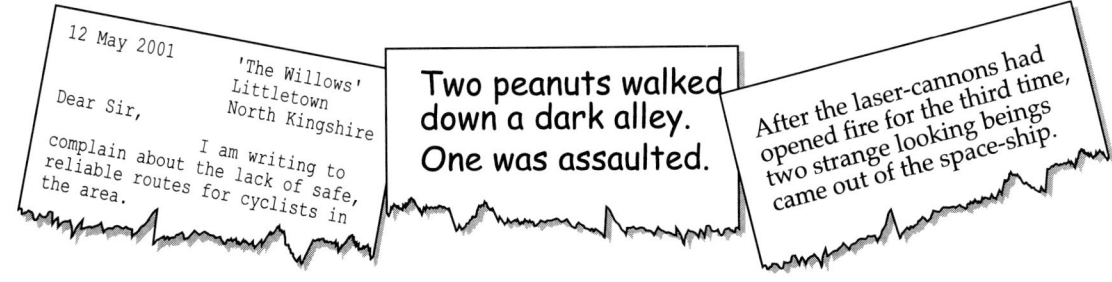

# What makes a good piece of writing to analyse, review, comment?

You now have an idea about what writing to analyse, review and comment is like. For homework, collect as many examples of these types of writing as you can. Look in newspapers and magazines. Look at textbooks. Look on the Internet. Look through the writing you do at school. Look at writing in other subjects, as well as in English.

Working in groups, look at the examples you have collected. Draw on your knowledge of non-fiction text-types. What **features** of writing to analyse, review and comment can you pick out? Do you think that some of your examples are better than others at getting their ideas across to their audience? Can you explain why?

Look for:

- how the writer catches the reader's attention at the start
- whether the writer addresses the reader with the second-person pronoun *you*
- how informal (more like speech) or formal (more like writing) the voice of the writer sounds
- how clearly the writer explains or describes what he or she is writing about
- how many examples or quotations the writer uses
- how the writer picks out the good and bad points, or strengths and weaknesses in what he or she is writing about
- how the writer gives his or her own opinion on the subject matter
- the main tense the writer uses and why he or she has used that tense
- the use of subordinate clauses
- the range of connectives which the writer uses
- when the writer starts new paragraphs.

As a class, make up a list of the features that you would expect to find in writing to analyse, review or comment. Record the list in your notebook. You might present what you have learnt as a wall display.

## How can you improve your own writing?

Collect two or three pieces of your own writing to analyse, review and comment. Talk to your partner about the features you have been discussing. Some things you will be doing already. What things do you need to improve?

On this page and the following page, there are grids which show in detail the things you need to do for a sound Level 5$^+$. There are a lot of things to think about, but don't worry. A lot of them you will already be good at, but some you will need to improve. The grids will help you think about them. If you are not sure about a feature, don't worry. Your teacher will be able to explain. You could also wait to see how the feature is used during the unit.

Copy the grids into your notebook. (It may also be possible for your teacher to photocopy them.) For each feature, put a tick in the box which applies to you. When you have finished, you will be able to see what you need to focus on in the rest of this unit. You will then be able to track your targets and improvements as you write.

| FEATURES OF WRITING | I can do this sometimes | I can usually do this | I need to improve this |
|---|---|---|---|
| I capture the reader's interest with a heading or opening sentence. | | | |
| I make sure that it's clear what pronouns refer back to. | | | |
| I know how to choose vocabulary to create a chatty, informal style. | | | |
| I know how to summarise the text. | | | |
| I use quotations to back up my ideas. | | | |
| I know how to explore ideas from words or phrases in a text. | | | |
| I end sentences with a full stop and start them with a capital letter. | | | |
| I write names with a capital letter. | | | |
| I use short or long sentences to create a mood that suits the text I am reviewing. | | | |
| I separate words, phrases and clauses in sentences with a single comma. | | | |
| I separate words, phrases and clauses in sentences with a pair of commas. | | | |

| FEATURES OF WRITING | I can do this sometimes | I can usually do this | I need to improve this |
|---|---|---|---|
| I choose when to separate a subordinate clause from a main clause with a comma. | | | |
| I use a range of connectives to begin subordinate clauses. | | | |
| I use a range of connectives to link sentences and paragraphs. | | | |
| I start a new paragraph to show a change in topic. | | | |
| I use a topic sentence for each paragraph. | | | |
| I develop the topic sentence by explaining in detail or by giving examples. | | | |
| I keep a list of the spellings and spelling patterns that I have trouble with. | | | |
| I check my drafts carefully for the spellings and patterns I have trouble with. | | | |

Now that you have reviewed your writing, record in your notebook the main things that you need to work on and improve. Keep checking your progress throughout the unit.

## Writing to analyse, review, comment: analysing and commenting on a poem

You can analyse, review and comment on any piece of writing, whether it is a whole long novel or a short poem. Whatever the text, the skills you need are the same. You need to review the text, which means telling the reader enough about the text so that they can understand it. You need to analyse the different elements of the text and you need to give your personal opinions or comment on the text. In this unit you will be writing a review of a poem.

Writing a review of a short piece of literature like a poem will be very useful in preparing you with the skills you will need to do well in your exams at the end of Key Stage 3 and in your GCSEs. You will need to write in a lively way that grabs and holds the reader's attention.

**Writing to analyse, review, comment**

## Looking at a review

### NEW UK CINEMA RELEASES

## The Fast and the Furious

| | |
|---|---|
| Starring: | Paul Walker, Vin Diesel, Michelle Rodriquez, Jordana Brewster, Rick Yune |
| Director: | Rob Cohen |
| Screen Writer: | Gary Scott Thompson, Erik Bergquist, David Ayer |
| Details: | 107 mins Cert 15 (Neal H. Moritz) |

### IN A NUTSHELL

On the darkened streets of LA, kids illegally race souped-up cars at speeds of over 150 mph. That's problem enough for the cops, but when a series of daring raids on moving trucks seems to be connected with the tribe of boy racers, they decide it's time to infiltrate the gangs ...

### FULL REVIEW

Now here's a delightful oddity – a movie that does exactly what it says on the tin. **The Fast and the Furious** is a mindless, hellaciously hectic, borderline irresponsible drag race of a movie that flattens the accelerator in the first few seconds and doesn't let it off until the final frame. And in Vin Diesel it invents the first genuine action hero since Bruce Willis paid a visit to Nakatomi Towers. In other words, it's a gas.

Lifting its title from an appropriately cheesy 1950s AIP racing flick (erstwhile creators of the classy likes of **I Was A Teenage Werewolf** and its plot from **Point Break**, Rob Cohen's movie is the kind of determinedly dimwitted popcorn entertainment that the big studios have been throwing hundreds of millions at this summer with, for the most part, limited success. Until now. And this, implausibly, from the man who made last year's execrable frat flick, **The Skulls**.

For a start TFATF has a plot – not a complex one, granted, but at least there's something close to a story. It has eye candy in the shape of dimwit bobby-dazzler Paul Walker (appropriately enough, a refugee from American soap **The Young And The Restless**) and Jordana Brewster. And it has Diesel, a unique brooding hulk of a man who looks as if he's either going to rip your head off or read you poetry.

But most of all it has car chases. Really fast ones.

Cars roar past – and even through – the camera at speeds of up to 170 mph, while in the hi-jack sequences they hurtle around and under speeding trucks – and, of course, smash into each other with satisfying regularity. In seamlessly interweaving top-notch CGI and incredible stuntwork, Cohen has delivered some of the finest auto-action ever put on screen.

### ANY GOOD?

★★★★

ADAM SMITH
Issue 148 October 2001

★★★

© Copyright EMAP Digital Limited 2001

# How do they do it?

Read the review of the film *The Fast and the Furious*. Then look at the commentary on the review and discuss the questions. There may be some words or ideas in the review that you don't understand. Don't worry about that at this stage.

Notice how:

- The review starts with a summary of the plot of the film, leaving you on a 'cliff hanger'. It tells you enough to understand what the film is about without giving away the ending. How much can you work out about the film from the first paragraph?

- The style is informal and chatty:
    - the vocabulary is informal: *kids, flick* (a slang word for a film) Can you find any other words or phrases that add to the informal chatty style?
    - the sentence structure makes the writer sound like he is talking to you: *Now here's a . . ., not a complex plot, granted, but at least . . .* Notice how he uses pairs of commas around words, like *granted*, which helps to give the text a chatty, spoken feel.
    - Later in the review, he starts with another phrase which adds to the chatty, spoken style: *For a start, TFATF has a plot . . .* Notice the comma dividing this phrase from the rest of the sentence. What would be the difference if the comma were left out?

- The first paragraph of the main review explains what sort of film it is: it is a fast moving, action packed film, about driving cars really fast, about people doing mad, irresponsible things, with a really good action hero.

- It uses vocabulary that fits with the subject matter of the film. There are lots of words about racing and speed and being irresponsible: *mindless, hectic, a drag race of a movie, flattens the accelerator*. These words help the reader understand the atmosphere of the film.

- It uses long breathless sentences with several clauses to give the reader a sense of the speed and breathlessness of the action in the film.

**The Fast and the Furious is a mindless, hellaciously hectic, borderline irresponsible drag race of a movie <u>that</u> flattens the accelerator in the first few seconds <u>and</u> doesn't let it off until the final frame.**

In the above sentence, the writer uses a relative pronoun (*that*) before the subordinate clause and a connective (*and*) to add a co-ordinate clause. Can you find any other long sentences that create the same effect? Notice how later in the review, the writer uses dashes instead of commas. Do you think this makes a difference to the 'feel' of the writing?

- The most common connective in the review is *and*. Normally, you are told not to use *and* too much, but to vary your connectives. Here, however, using *and* makes all the ideas in the film rush together in one breathless stream of ideas, imitating the speed and breathlessness of the film. Do you think this works or would the review would be better with a wider range of connectives?

# Writing to analyse, review, comment

- It tells you a little bit about the main characters so that you know who is in the film. It tells you who the actors are. Why do you think it does this?

- It uses a short paragraph to make the main good point of the film stand out. Notice how the second phrase in the paragraph is not a complete sentence: *Really fast ones*. There is no verb. That adds to the informal, chatty style and helps make the point stand out that the film has really good, fast car chases.

- It gives most detail about the strongest point of the movie; the car action. As a reader, you know that the best bit of the film is the car chases.

- The opinion of the writer is very clear at the end. He clearly likes the film a lot!

## It's your turn

You are going to write a review of a poem called *A Case of Murder* by Vernon Scannell. Before you write your review, you will need to have a good detailed understanding of the poem. You will need to analyse the poem for yourself. This means looking closely at all the different details and parts of the poem and having your own ideas about the pictures, thoughts or feelings we get from words and phrases in the poem.

Read the poem below and on page 72. Then, in pairs or groups, do the activities that follow.

## A Case of Murder

They should not have left him there alone,
Alone that is except for the cat.
He was only nine, not old enough
To be left alone in a basement flat,
Alone, that is, except for the cat.
A dog would have been a different thing,
A big gruff dog with slashing jaws,
But a cat with round eyes mad as gold,

Plump as a cushion with tucked-in paws –
Better have left him with a fair-sized rat!
But what they did was leave him with a cat.
He hated that cat; he watched it sit,
A buzzing machine of soft black stuff,
He sat and watched and he hated it,
Snug in its fur, hot blood in a muff,
And its mad gold stare and the way it sat
Crooning dark warmth: he loathed all that.
So he took Daddy's stick and he hit the cat.
Then quick as a sudden crack in glass
It hissed, back flash, to a hiding place
In the dust and dark beneath the couch,
And he followed the grin on his new-made face,
A wide-eyed, frightened snarl of a grin,
And he took the stick and he thrust it in,
Hard and quick in the furry dark,
The black fur squealed and he felt his skin
Prickle with sparks of dry delight.
Then the cat again came into sight,
Shot for the door that wasn't quite shut,

But the boy, quick too, slammed fast the door:
The cat, half-through, was cracked like a nut
And the soft black thud wad dumped on the floor.
Then the boy was suddenly terrified
And he bit his knuckles and cried and cried;
But he had to do something with the dead thing there.
His eyes squeezed beads of salty prayer
But the wound of fear gaped wide and raw;
He dared not touch the thing with his hands
So he fetched a spade and shovelled it
And dumped the load of heavy fur
In the spidery cupboard under the stair
Where it's been for years, and though it died
It's grown in the cupboard and its hot low purr
Grows slowly louder year by year:
There'll not be a corner for the boy to hide
When the cupboard swells and all sides split
And the huge black cat pads out of it.

*Vernon Scannell*

## Getting to know the poem

- What is the story of the poem? Re-read the poem and write a summary of what happens in the poem in about five to ten lines.
- Underline any words or phrases that describe the cat. Discuss for each phrase what picture or idea they give you of the cat. Make a table to write down your ideas like this:

| Plump as a cushion with tucked-in paws | *This gives me a picture of the cat as really fat and squashy, like a cushion and you can't see his paws because they are hidden underneath his fat body.* |
|---|---|
| Hot blood in a muff | |
| A buzzing machine of soft black stuff | |
| Crooning dark warmth | |

- Now underline any words or phrases that describe the boy or his feelings. Discuss what he is feeling at different points in the poem and what causes those feelings. Then make another table to record your ideas:

| He ... watched [the cat] and he hated it | *Maybe he hated the cat because it was all warm and happy, purring away, while he was only nine and had been left alone. I think he felt jealous of the cat.* |
|---|---|
| His skin prickle with sparks of dry delight | *He seems to be enjoying hurting the cat. I think this is because ...* |
| His eyes squeezed beads of salty prayer | |

- Next, discuss these questions about the ending of the poem and the poem overall. Make brief notes of your ideas so that you can use them later.

  - What do you learn in the poem about the boy's parents? How do you think they treat him? How do you think they treat the cat? Why do you think the poet mentions *Daddy's stick*?
  - Why do you think the boy seems to enjoy hurting the cat?
  - How do you think he feels at the end?
  - What different meanings could the ending have? What do you think the poet wants us to think happens at the end?
  - Who do you think is most to blame for the murder: the boy or his parents?
  - Do you think the writer wants us to feel angry or sorry for the boy?
  - Look at the statements below about what sort of poem *A Case of Murder* is. Discuss which of them you think are most true. Give your reasons.

*The poem is like a short horror story written as a poem.*
*The poem is a sad story about child abuse.*
*The poem is for people who like cats.*
*The poem is to teach a message about cruelty to animals.*
*The poem is a funny story with a serious message.*

- Now in your own words, explain what sort of poem you think *A Case of Murder* is.

You should now have a good detailed understanding of the poem and are ready to start writing your review.

## Planning your review

You will need to plan your review in the following sections:

- an introduction to the sort of poem this poem is (a funny poem? A comedy? A poem with a message?) and a summary of the story of the poem
- an analysis of the way the cat is presented by the writer
- an analysis of the way the writer presents the boy and his feelings as they change through the poem
- an analysis of the different interpretations of what the ending could mean
- your comment on the poem overall.

Remember, analysing means looking closely at all the different details and parts of the poem and having your own ideas about the pictures, thoughts or feelings we get from words and phrases in the poem.

For each of these sections, write four or five ideas for what you will say in your review. Don't write in whole sentences; these are just notes which you will use later.

## Writing your review

To write a good review at Level 5⁺ you will need to demonstrate your ability to:

- hold the reader's attention by:
  - your use of vocabulary which suits the subject matter of the review
  - your use of varied sentence lengths for effect
- use a wide range of connectives
- use single and double commas to separate subordinate clauses
- give a detailed analysis of the text
- use evidence to back up or develop your ideas
- present different viewpoints
- give your opinion about the poem.

These next activities will help you develop these skills.

## The opening paragraph

This paragraph is very important. You have to grab the reader's attention to make them read the rest of the review. You have to tell enough of the story of the poem so that they can understand what you are saying without reading the poem for themselves. You also have to explain to the reader what sort of poem *A Case of Murder* is. Is it a comedy? A poem with a message? A horror story? A poem about parents and children? You can give the reader an idea about the sort of poem this is by the sorts of vocabulary and sentences you use to introduce it, like the writer did in the review of the film, *The Fast and the Furious*.

Look at these two first sentences.

*'A Case of Murder' is a very interesting poem about a boy who is in a flat and who kills a cat and the cat comes back to get him or does it?*

*A black cat. A small boy. No parents. A basement flat. All the ingredients you need for a brutal story of jealousy, hatred, violent death and, finally, terrifying guilt.*

- Which best grabs your attention?
- Which best gives the impression that this is a poem about murder and not romance and roses?
- Will you use short sentences to create a tense, 'on the edge of your seat' atmosphere?
- Or will you use long sentences to create a calm, peaceful, but 'anything might happen' atmosphere?
- What describing words will you include to make it very clear that this is not a sunny, happy poem, but one about violence and death, jealousy and guilt?

Look at this list of adjectives: Which would you use to describe the poem, the boy, the flat, the parents or the cat? Which would you not use?

*Tragic, cruel, calm, tortured, loved, beautiful, hated, bleak, cold, funny, lonely, careless, violent, brutal, confusing, surprising, gentle, heart-warming, chilling, hair-raising, romantic.*

Remember how the writer of the review of *The Fast and the Furious* uses a chatty, informal style to show that it is not a serious film, and to make his review appeal to younger readers. You could use a similar style, or you might want to use a more serious formal style to show that *A Case of Murder* is a serious poem.

Aim to use sentence starters that will keep your summary moving. Use words like: *suddenly, while, despite the fact that, as, when, just then, finally*. Don't forget to check if you need a comma when you start with a word or phrase like *suddenly, however, just then, later*.

Now draft the first paragraph, telling the reader what sort of poem this is and summarising the story of the poem.

## Analysing the poem

- You have to analyse the way the writer has presented the cat and the boy.
- You have to present different possible opinions about the boy or the cat.
- You have to use quotations as evidence to back up your ideas. You have to use the words and phrases in the poem to explore in more detail your ideas about the cat and the boy.
- You need to write using co-ordinate and subordinate clauses, to make your sentences more complex, and single or double commas where necessary to separate the clauses.

Look at this example to show you how to analyse the way the poet has written about the boy and the cat.

*The boy, when he realised he had killed the cat, was scared. He writes, 'His eyes squeezed beads of salty prayer'. The phrase 'squeezed beads' gives me a picture of the boy standing there, with tear drops running out of the corner of his eyes. The words 'salty prayer' makes me think the boy is praying. The word 'salty' makes you think he can taste the saltiness in the tears. While you could say that he is praying for the cat to come back to life, I think he is praying that his parents don't find out, because he is scared of the consequences.*

In this paragraph, notice how the writer:

- starts with a clear topic sentence to tell the reader what the paragraph will be about
- talks about individual words and phrases from the poem, not just whole sentences
- gives different views about what the words might mean
- uses subordinate clauses: *when he realised ...*, *with tear drops ...* and *While ... he is praying ...*
- uses a pair of commas around a subordinate clause in the middle of a sentence, to show that the clause is adding extra information to the sentence
- uses a single comma to divide the subordinate clause from the rest of the sentence.

You need a long paragraph or two about the cat and maybe three paragraphs about the boy and his feelings at the beginning, the middle and the end of the poem.

Use these phrases to help you write:

*The writer says ...*
*The poet describes ...*
*Next, he explains, ...*
*Later, he says, ...*
*The word ... gives me a picture of ...*
*The phrase ... makes me think ...*
*Some people might say ... but I think ...*
*When he says ..., I think it shows ...*
*The phrase ... could mean, but on the other hand, ...*
*Although ...*

Remember to write a clear topic sentence at the beginning of each paragraph to tell the reader what you writing about. Try to use a range of connectives, and subordinate clauses, with commas marking the subordinate clauses off from the rest of the sentence.

## Your last paragraph

This is where you give your opinion about the poem. But remember, your task as a reviewer is to make the reader go and read the poem for him or herself, so that they can then form their own opinions about it.

As with your opening paragraph, you could make this concluding paragraph more informal. You could talk more directly to your reader, asking them questions for example, or you could finish with a more chatty style.

Look at these two examples of sentences that start a final paragraph.

*I think the poem is very sad and I thought the boy was very cruel. You should read this poem and see what you think of him.*

*So there you have it. A cruel killer, who should be locked up? Or a sad and neglected child who desperately needs a little bit of love and attention? And what about the end? Is it a ghost? A guilty conscience? Or some nightmare come back from the dead? I thought ... but that's only my opinion. Get hold of a copy of this thought-provoking poem for yourself ...*

Which do you think is most effective in summing up the poem, in giving the reader the writer's opinion and in getting them to go off and read the poem?

Now write your own final paragraph, summing up your own opinion, but also persuading the reader that they need to go and get a copy of the poem to read for themselves.

## Revising your draft

When you've finished your draft, work with a partner to revise it before you write your final version. Check over the following features:

- Is it **clear** what you have said? Ask your partner to read your draft. Ask them to mark places where they aren't sure what you mean. Ask them to mark places where the sentences don't follow on clearly.
- Have you ended each sentence with a **full stop**? (Count the number of sentences you have written in each paragraph. Write the number in the margin. Then count the number of full stops. The numbers should be the same!)
- Do all your sentences **begin with a capital letter**? (Underline the first word of each sentence. Has it got a capital letter?)
- Have you used **capital letters for names**? (Underline each name in what you have written. Put a ring round the first letter. Is it a capital?)

And:

- Have you used a **single comma** to **mark off words and phrases** from the rest of the sentence? (For example, *suddenly, just then, ...*)
- Have you separated some of your **subordinate and co-ordinate clauses** from main clauses with **commas**?
- Have you put **pairs of commas** around clauses or phrases dropped into the middle of a sentence?

And:

- Have you **summarised** the poem so that a reader who does not know the poem will understand what you are saying?
- Have you used **vocabulary** which fits with the mood of the poem?
- Have you used slang or chatty words to create an informal style?
- Have you included **quotations**?
- Have you explored the ideas you get from the words or phrases you have quoted?
- Have you given your own **opinions**?

And:

- Have you used a **topic sentence** when you start a new paragraph? (Underline the topic sentence in each paragraph.)
- Have you **developed** the topic sentence in the rest of the paragraph?

And finally:

- Check your draft carefully for the **spelling patterns** you know you have trouble with. (Use your spelling list to remind you.)

When you are ready, review your progress using the grids from pages 67 and 68. What features of writing have you improved? The more improvements you have made, the closer you are to a sound Level 5⁺.

Now write the final draft of your review. Make sure that your handwriting and overall presentation are as neat as possible.

# And you could try ...

## Writing a book review

Choose a book you have read recently on your own or in class. You will need to explain briefly what the story is about, who the characters were, where and when it is set. Say how it is similar to other books by that author or in that genre (or type) of story.

To explain your opinions about what was good or bad about the book, you will need to write a separate paragraph about what you liked about the characters and the plot. Did the characters make you want to find out what happened to them? Did they make you feel angry or sorry for them? How was the plot gripping or believable? Did the plot make you want to turn the pages? What was the most exciting part? Explain what you liked about the style and the language. Was there enough description to help you picture the events of the story? Were the chapters about the right length?

Explain what sort of reader would like the book and why. As with your review of *A Case of Murder*, remember to:

- start your review with a good first sentence to grab the reader's attention
- decide if you are going to use an informal, chatty style with slang, or a more formal style
- use well-chosen vocabulary to hold the reader's attention and to give the reader the atmosphere or mood of the book; if it is a horror story, use lots of dark, scary adjectives. If it is a romance, use lots of happy, sunny, romantic ones
- make sure you include lots of quotations. Explore the quotations using the same phrases you used in this unit
- use a range of connectives to vary the way you start and join sentences
- make sure you use a comma or a pair of commas where necessary to separate clauses.

You could also write a review of a TV programme, film or video that you have watched. You could also write about a poem or an extract from a play or book that you have read or studied in class in the way that you will have to do in your exams in Year 9 or for your GCSEs. If you do this, make sure you:

- look carefully at the question to see what exactly you are being asked to write about
- avoid slang or chatty vocabulary. Use a serious formal style in exams.
- keep to the formula of **Point, Quote, Comment**:
  - **Make a point**. Explain an idea you have that will help answer the question.
  - **Find a quote**. Copy a sentence, phrase or idea from the text which backs up or explains your point. Always put the quote in speech marks, also known as quotation marks.
  - **Comment on the quote**. Use the quote as a way of expanding your point. Find a single word to write about or link your point to a point you made earlier.
- remember your audience is the examiner who wants to know how well you understand the question and the text, and how well you can explain your ideas, using and explaining quotation in a fluent and accurate style, with good complex sentences and well-chosen vocabulary. Easy really!